Knitting
Handbook

Knitting
Handbook

THUNDER BAY
P·R·E·S·S

San Diego, California

Thunder Bay Press
An imprint of the Advantage Publishers Group
THUNDER BAY 5880 Oberlin Drive, San Diego, CA 92121-4794
P·R·E·S·S www.thunderbaybooks.com

Library of Congress Cataloging-in-Publication Data

Knitting handbook.
    p. cm.
  Includes index
  ISBN 1-59223-175-6
  1. Knitting. I. Thunder Bay Press.

TT820.K6995 2004
746.43'2--dc22

2003060380

QUMKSH

Manufactured in Singapore by Pica Digital Pte Ltd
Printed in China by CT Printing Ltd.

1 2 3 4 5 08 07 06 05 04

CONTENTS

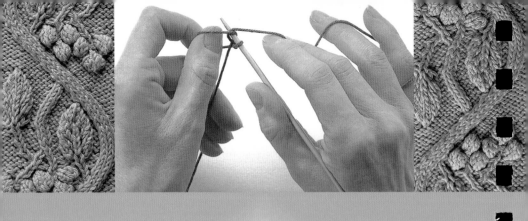

INTRODUCTION

Knitting is the art of constructing a flexible fabric from a notionally continuous thread. The surface of the fabric can be smooth or textured, and the knitted pieces can be flat or tubular, straight or shaped, in infinite variety. All you need to know to get started is how to hold the yarn and needles, how to cast on and off, and the two basic stitches: knit and purl.

Knitting is the art of constructing a flexible fabric from a notionally continuous thread. The surface of the fabric can be smooth or textured, and the knitted pieces can be flat or tubular, straight or shaped, in infinite variety. All you need to know to get started is how to hold the yarn and needles, how to cast on and off, and the two basic stitches : knit and purl. When you're familiar with shapings and have tried out more techniques, there's the "Knitting with Color" section to explore, with its mixture of old and new stitch patterns. Then browse through "Design Your Own Knits" to gain the confidence to create knitting that's all your own work.

To start knitting, all you need is a pair of needles and some yarn. But before you cast on the first stitch, it would be helpful to know what you are going to make.

You can, of course, buy patterns. They can be found in books like this one, magazines, knit kits, and the leaflets produced by the yarn spinners. But you'll probably come up with ways to adapt these patterns—or even have

These richly patterned Peruvian hats are recent examples of an old tradition.

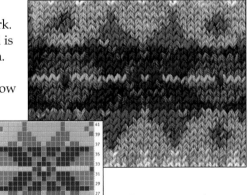

Color patterns are shown as color charts.

ideas for completely new patterns of your own.

Knitting is an ideal hobby in today's busy world: It can be laid aside and picked up again at any time, requires little special equipment, and is easy to carry around with you. The new hand-knitter will find today's

Ideas for motifs can be found everywhere—from old prints to antique textiles. (See examples above and at top of next page.)

Some hand-knitted fabrics are more stable than others, some are more dense, some are open, some expand, and some contract, so it's essential to consider the use that the knitting will be put to when selecting yarn and stitch. Different yarns have been used throughout this book to suggest the characteristics of various stitches, but trial and error is really the best way to test the suitability of a stitch for a particular purpose. However, don't be inhibited or imagine that there are rules that can't be broken. Many mistakes turn out to be happy accidents, and many a new stitch pattern is the result of an old one being bungled!

chunky and bulky yarns ideal for achieving quick results, and the new generation of microfiber yarns unsurpassed for comfort and practicality. The wide range of beautiful colors and textures, styles, and patterns currently available will surely inspire you to pick up your needles, and with the help of this book you will be able to follow any pattern. You can then create original garments for yourself and your family by choosing your own color combinations and adding your own individual touches.

As you pursue your new craft and the basic skills become familiar, you will find that knitting can be relaxing and satisfying, as well as productive. Enjoy the colors and textures, let the rhythm of the needles take over your fingers, and watch your work grow in your hands.

The majority of designs in this book are easy to follow and a large chart may be based on repetition rather than complexity. So don't be afraid to tackle something just because it's large in scale or looks complicated. Enjoy every step of the process, and happy knitting!

EQUIPMENT & MATERIALS

You don't need complicated or expensive equipment to learn to knit–just knitting needles and yarn. As you progress in the craft, you can collect more equipment and enjoy using all kinds of yarn.

Equipment

To experiment with different yarns and gauges, you'll need knitting needles in different sizes, a cable needle for working cable-stitch patterns, and double-pointed needles, or a circular needle if you want to try knitting in the round. When you're ready to knit a garment, you'll need a tape measure or ruler, stitch holders, scissors, a tapestry or wool needle, and maybe a few other pieces of equipment. Feeling the yarn as it slips through your fingers is one of the pleasures of knitting. Add to that enjoyment by exploring a whole range of yarns, from fine and smooth to bulky and textured, in synthetic blends and natural fibers.

ESSENTIAL EQUIPMENT

Knitting needles are an investment because you'll use them time and time again. Look after your needles carefully and they'll last for years, but when the points are damaged or the needles are bent, it's time to throw them out and buy new ones.

Pairs of needles come in a variety of lengths and sizes, and are used to produce flat knitting. The size of the needle is determined by the yarn thickness and required tension. The metric size of a needle indicates the width of the diameter. The chart on page 13 shows metric sizes with equivalent American and U.K. sizes.

DOUBLE-POINTED NEEDLES

Sets of double-pointed needles produce seamless knitting for socks or stockings. They come in the same range of sizes as pairs of needles

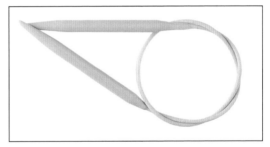

Circular needles

and are usually sold and used in sets of four.

CIRCULAR NEEDLES

Circular needles are used either in place of pairs of needles or in place of sets of needles. A circular needle is a pair of short needles attached to each other by a length of nylon cord. They come in the full range of sizes and also in different lengths. It is important to use the correct length when working seamless knitting.

CABLE NEEDLES

Cable needles are short, double-pointed needles used for working cables. Normally they are sold in packs of two containing a large and small size. The size nearest to the main needle size should be used.

NEEDLE GAUGE

A needle gauge is used to determine the size of a needle. While pairs of needles are usually marked with the size, sets of needles and circular needles are often unmarked.

STITCH HOLDERS

Stitch holders are used to hold stitches when they are removed from the needle but not cast off. A piece of contrasting colored yarn can also be threaded through stitches on a stitch holder. A safety pin can be used for holding a few stitches.

WOOL SEWING NEEDLE

Wool sewing needles are used for sewing up finished knitted items. A wool sewing needle should have a large eye and a blunted point.

CROCHET HOOK

Crochet hooks are useful for picking up dropped stitches or attaching decorations such as tassels.

OTHER EQUIPMENT

A tape measure or ruler is needed to measure the work in progress. A row counter allows one to keep count of the rows while knitting. It is especially useful for working shapings. However, using paper and pencil can be just as effective.

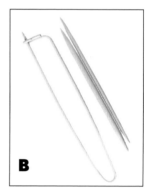

A Crochet hook

B Stitch holder and cable needles

B

A

NEEDLE
size chart

Metric	U.K	U.S.
2mm	14	00
2.25mm	13	0
2.5mm	–	–
2.75mm	12	1
3mm	11	2
3.25mm	10	3
3.5mm	–	–
3.75mm	9	4
4mm	8	5
4.5mm	7	6
5mm	6	7
5.5mm	5	8
6mm	4	9
6.5mm	3	10
7mm	2	10½
7.5mm	1	11
8mm	0	12
9mm	00	13
10mm	000	15

Pairs of needles are made in a variety of lengths, ranging from around 10 in. to 16 in. Most knitting needles are aluminum, usually with a pearl-gray finish, though some are nickel plated. Larger-size needles are made of plastic to reduce their weight. Bamboo needles are a flexible alternative.

Double-pointed needles are sold in sets of four or five, and in several lengths. They were traditionally made of steel, but aluminum needles are more common now, with bamboo and plastic in some sizes.

Circular needles are simply two short needle ends joined by a flexible nylon or plastic cord. The length of a circular needle is measured from needle tip to needle tip. Most sizes are in lengths from 16 in. to 47 in.

The most useful tape measures have both inches and centimeters on the same side so that you can compare measurements.

Materials

The yarns available to the hand-knitter today include many varieties of color, thickness, and texture. When used imaginatively, these can create the kind of high fashion garments usually only seen in the pages of magazines. However, the range of choices can be confusing to the knitter. Some of this confusion arises from the great variety of terms used to describe the yarn thickness, the spinning process, and the various fibers used to make knitting yarns.

YARN THICKNESS

All knitting patterns, whether commercially produced or homemade, are worked out on the basis of a tension square that alters according to the yarn thickness, the size of the needles, and the stitch pattern. The tension of a piece of knitting is the number of stitches and rows needed to knit a measured square. It is usually only necessary to have an accurate way of knowing the thickness of various types of yarn if you want to substitute one yarn for another or use different yarns in the same garment—for instance, when making stripes. The only sure way of doing this is to knit a tension square in the chosen yarn and check that it matches the tension given for the original yarn.

There are several terms used by the yarn spinners to denote the thickness of a yarn, but these are very vague and differ from spinner to spinner. It is better to refer to a yarn as knitting to a certain tension rather than being of a certain thickness. Yarn spinners often state the recommended tension and needle size on the ball band label.

Listed on the opposite page are the terms most commonly used to describe yarn thicknesses, together with their approximate corresponding tensions. However, even within each grouping the manufacturers' recommended tensions can vary greatly. All the tensions given below are for 4 in. squares, worked in stocking stitch.

Aran thick (also called triple thick or sportswool): 18 sts and 24 rows on No. 6 needles.
Mohair thick: 16 sts and 22 rows on No. 8 needles; however, some mohair yarns knit to an equivalent of double knit or chunky yarn.
Chunky: 14 sts and 22 rows on No. 10 needles.

Some yarns are even thicker than chunky, but these are usually very individual and, unless an exact tension match can be obtained, it is not a good idea to try using other yarns in their place, as variations in tension over thick yarns cause a much greater difference in the finished size of a garment than differences in tension over finer yarns.

YARN SPINNING

Yarns are made from natural and man-made fibers of various lengths. The two terms to describe these lengths are:

Filaments

Filaments are very long fibers. Man-made filament fibers can be made to any length, but they are usually cut into shorter staple lengths before being spun to form hand-knitting yarns. The only natural filament fiber is silk.

Staples

Staples are comparatively short fibers. To form a yarn that is suitable for knitting, they must be twisted together in one continuous strand of the required thickness. This continuous strand is called a single yarn. A single yarn is usually twisted together with others; this is called "plying" or "folding." From this come the terms "2-ply," "3-ply," etc., to denote the number of single yarns (or any thickness) plied together. The twisting process used to form yarns is known as "spinning."

Here are some of the terms used for the various ways of spinning yarns together.

Bouclé is a knobbly yarn created by spinning one or more very fine, taut yarns together with a thicker, softer yarn, thus forming a random pattern of "lumps" along the length of yarn.

Brushed yarns are made from fibers with a long stable that can be brushed to produce a furry effect.

Chenille is made from fine, hard yarns, spun together, with other, softer fibers anchored into this "cord" and sticking out at an angle to it.

Crepe is a very highly twisted yarn.

Gimp is a variation of bouclé yarn, with a more even appearance.

Loop is another variation of bouclé yarn. The lumps formed are made of little loops of yarn.

Lopi is a thick single yarn; it is not very strong.

Slub is an uneven-thickness yarn, made by spinning alternatively tight and loose.

Spiral is a core yarn, very taut and fine, wrapped around with a thicker yarn so that the core yarn is hidden.

Worsted is a smooth yarn where all the fibers are fairly long and run parallel to each other. Most ordinary knitting yarns are worsted.

YARN FIBERS

Yarns for hand-knitting are made from a variety of fibers, both natural and man-made, and sometimes, for reasons of strength or design, they are combined to form yarns made of mixed fibers. Each different fiber, whether man-made or natural, has its advantages and disadvantages.

NATURAL FIBERS
The wool family

Wool is obtained from the fleece of a sheep. It comes in a variety of qualities, depending on the type of sheep, its condition, the climate in which it is reared, etc. High-quality wool has a short staple, but is not so strong or elastic as the poorer qualities.

Lambswool, which is very soft and fine, is the wool from the first shearing of a lamb.

Advantages of wool

It has good insulating properties, is very absorbent, holds its shape well, and is very hard-wearing.

Disadvantages of wool

It has a tendency to shrink, it can be itchy, and takes a long time to dry. Other yarns in the wool family that come from the fleece of animals are:

Alpaca comes from the alpaca and the llama, both found in South America. It is a fairly silky fiber, but the cheaper alpaca yarns can be very itchy.

Angora comes from the fleece of the Angora rabbit and is very soft and fluffy, but not very strong. It is usually mixed with wool when spinning to give extra strength.

Cashmere comes from goats found in the Kashmir region of the Himalayas. The yarn is very soft, warm, and lightweight. However, it is very expensive and not very strong.

Mohair comes from a goat originally bred in Turkey. As they are very expensive, most mohair yarns are mixed with other fibers. The classic fluffy mohair look comes from brushing. It can be very itchy.

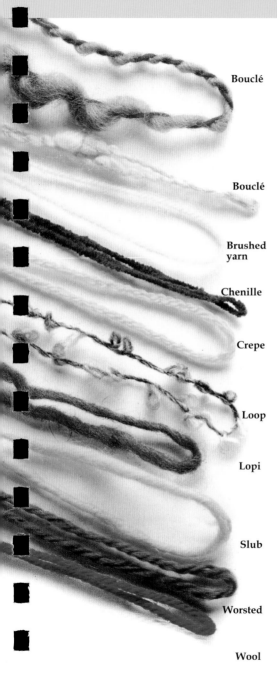

Bouclé

Bouclé

Brushed yarn

Chenille

Crepe

Loop

Lopi

Slub

Worsted

Wool

Silk is the only natural filament fiber and is taken from the cocoons of various types of silkworm. A very strong fiber with a smooth, shiny appearance, it is warm in winter and cool in summer. It mixes well with other fibers. The silkworm cocoons have to be unwound by hand to provide the silk filament, so it is very expensive. However, spun silk, made from broken lengths of this filament, is much cheaper.

Tussah silk or wild silk, produced from an undomesticated silkworm, is resilient to dyeing and bleaching, so is often used in its natural brown color. It is a coarse, uneven yarn.

Cotton comes from the staple fibers of the seed of a cotton plant. High-quality cotton, made from the long staples, is very soft, strong, and expensive. Although very strong, cotton has little elasticity. It is, however, useful for summer wear as it is a good conductor of heat. Cotton is sometimes blended with other fibers such as wool.

Linen is made from the long staple fibers obtained from the stalks of the flax plant. It is much stronger than cotton, especially when wet, but also has very little elasticity. Because of their naturally uneven fiber, linen knitting yarns are usually slubbed. Linen has a tendency to shrink.

Viscose rayon is produced from the cellulose extracted from wood pulp.

Knitting yarns made from viscose rayon are often very shiny and for this reason it is often used as a substitute for silk. It is, however, a fairly weak fabric that needs careful washing and has only a little elasticity. On the plus side, viscose rayon is a fairly heavy yarn and garments made from it drape well.

Nylon, also known as polyamide, is a synthetic yarn made from petroleum-based chemicals. It is very strong and elastic but not very comfortable to wear in hot weather. Nylon can serve many useful purposes when it is mixed with other fibers.

Acrylic is made from a type of plastic. It has various trade names that are in common use, the main ones being Acrilan, Orlon, and Courtelle. It is often used as a substitute for wool, but has a tendency to lose its shape and special care must be taken when washing, as acrylic garments tend to crease easily.

Polyester is a synthetic fiber, similar to nylon but less shiny. It is fairly strong and elastic and does not crease easily.

UNUSUAL YARNS

A knitting yarn can be any material that has a length considerably longer than its width. It would, in theory, be possible to knit with metal wire spaghetti, sewing cotton, etc., but garments made from those substances would not be very practical at all.

The essence of creative design is the ability to "break all the rules" and still produce a garment with all the required correct properties. For instance, it should be flexible enough to fit around a body, it should hold its shape well, it should be washable, and it should feel comfortable.

It is also possible to create one's own yarns by knitting two or more

---

IDEAS
FOR CREATIVE DESIGNS

• Cut lengths of "fabric" knotted or sewn together, e.g., chiffon, tweed, lurex, fur, leather, foam, tinfoil, hessian, PVC, Vilene, etc.

• Bias binding, ribbon, lace, fringing, and other bought "tapes."

• Plastic tubing, garden string, lengths of chain, and other items found in hardware stores.

• Colorful gift wrap ribbons, tinsel, etc.

different yarns together or by attaching objects to the length of yarn and causing them to drop to the front of the work when knitting. This is often done with sequins and beads, but you could try paper clips, shells, homemade clay or acrylic shapes, buttons, curtain rings, and the like. You can also create your own bouclé yarn by knotting it. When mixing yarns together, try using yarns not only of different colors, but also of different textures, e.g., mix cotton bouclé with mohair, chunky wool with rayon or silk, or baby yarns with lurex.

When using these more unusual yarns, any needle size can be used, provided that the resulting knitted fabric is fairly firm so that the garment will hold its shape well. You will obviously have to write your own patterns in order to use your yarn.

WASHING KNITTED GARMENTS

Follow the instructions given on the ball band label of the yarn that has been used. Where two or more yarns have been used, the washing instructions for the yarn with the lowest temperature wash and iron should be used.

If you have created your own yarn or are unsure of the properties of a garment, try washing the tension square to see how it reacts.

Some garments specifically require dry cleaning, but most can be washed in cool water. Do not iron a garment that you are unsure about.

After washing, knitted fabrics should be dried flat in order to preserve their shape. If necessary, they should be pulled back into the correct shape when laying them out for drying.

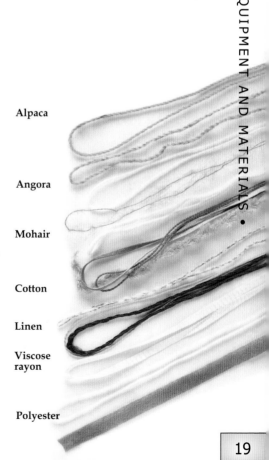

Alpaca

Angora

Mohair

Cotton

Linen

Viscose rayon

Polyester

BASIC SKILLS

This section of the book introduces you to all the basic knitting skills you will need to get started. Work through the steps slowly and thoroughly to learn how to hold the needles, cast on stitches, and work various stitch combinations. By doing this you will discover the most comfortable, quickest, and most enjoyable way to start knitting.

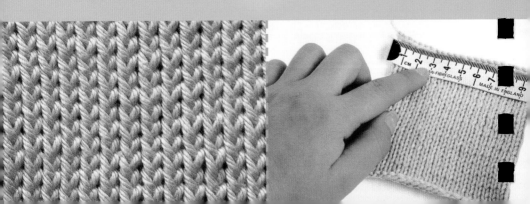

Holding the Yarn

There are many ways to hold and control the yarn and needles, but there is no one correct method. Experiment until you find one that suits you. Start by running the yarn through your fingers—see how the holds shown below all have the yarn over the forefinger, ready to make a stitch.

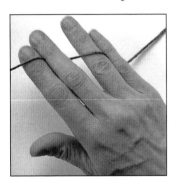 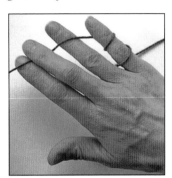

To feed the yarn onto the needle evenly, run it through and around your fingers, leaving the fingertips free to manipulate the needles and control the yarn.

The simplest method (above left) is to slip the yarn over and under the fingers of the right hand. Wrapping the yarn around the little finger tensions it more firmly (above right).

If you want to hold the yarn in your left hand, try taking it over, under, and around the fingers (below left). Alternatively, wrap the yarn around the little finger, then under and over the other fingers (below right).

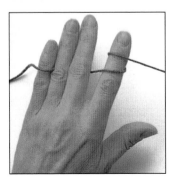 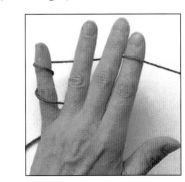

Holding the Needles

Some knitters hold the right needle like a pen. Others hold it overhand like a knife.
With the free needle, or pen, hold, the needles used are as short as is practical
and the weight of the knitting on the right needle is supported by the hand
and wrist. With the fixed needle, or knife, hold, long needles are used and
the right needle is tucked under the arm for support.

If you're a beginner, try these steps using medium-size needles and a smooth, medium-weight pure wool yarn.

FIXED NEEDLE

With your right hand, pick up the needle, hold it overhand like a knife, and tuck the end of the needle under your arm. Take the other needle in your left hand, holding it lightly over the top. Practice moving the left needle against the right. When you start knitting, you'll find you can let go of the needle every time you make a stitch.

FREE NEEDLE

With your right hand, pick up a needle and hold it like a pen. Take the other needle in your left hand, holding it lightly with your hand over the top. Try moving the needles forward and back with your fingertips, keeping your elbows relaxed at your sides. When you cast on and start knitting, don't drop the right needle to manipulate the yarn, but support it in the crook of your thumb and use your forefinger to control the yarn.

LEFT HAND

With your right hand, pick up the needle and hold it like a pen. With your left hand, pick up the other needle. When knitting, hold the yarn taut with the left hand while hooking or catching it with the point of the right-hand needle.

Casting On

The first step in beginning any piece of knitting is to cast on some stitches. Here are some of the most useful ways to cast on.

The two-needle cable cast on makes a strong edge with a ropelike twist, but it's not very elastic. The thumb cast on uses just one needle and is very versatile. It's very compatible with ribs due to its elasticity. Used with garter stitch, it's indistinguishable from the rest of the knitting as it is, in effect, a knit row. The loop cast on also uses one needle; it's simple and useful for buttonholes.

SLIP KNOT

Putting a slip knot on the needle makes your first stitch. You can coil the yarn around your fingers or lay it flat.

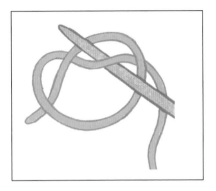

1 Coil the yarn into a loop, bring forward the strand underneath, and insert the needle as shown above.

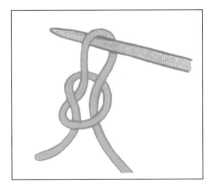

2 Pull one end to tighten the knot, then gently pull the other end of the yarn to close the knot up to the needle. You're ready to cast on.

TIP

• A less robust cast on is made if you take the needle into the stitch instead of between stitches. This edge is useful for hems.

CABLE CAST ON

This cast on is made by knitting a stitch, then transferring it from the right to the left needle.

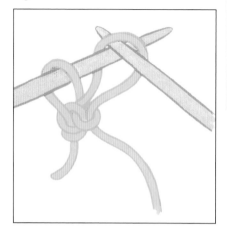

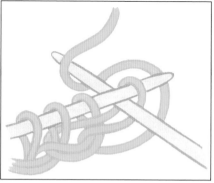

2 From now on, insert the right needle between the stitches each time. Transfer each new stitch to the left needle as before.

1 Leaving a short end, make a slipknot on one needle. Holding this needle in the left hand, insert the other needle into the front of the slip stitch. Take the yarn around the right needle and pull through a stitch, then transfer it to the left needle.

LOOP CAST ON

Tension the yarn carefully for this very basic cast on.

Leaving a short end, make a slipknot on the needle. Tension the yarn in your left hand and make a loop around your thumb.

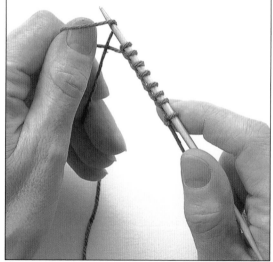

Insert the needle in the loop, slip your thumb out, and gently pull the yarn to make a stitch on the needle.

THUMB CAST ON
Using this method, you simply knit each stitch of your thumb.

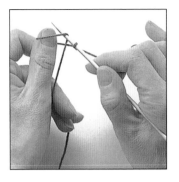

1 Measure off about three times the length of the edge to be cast on and make a slipknot on the needle. Hold the needle and yarn from the ball in your right hand.

2 Tensioning the other end in your left hand, make a loop around your thumb and insert the right needle in the loop.

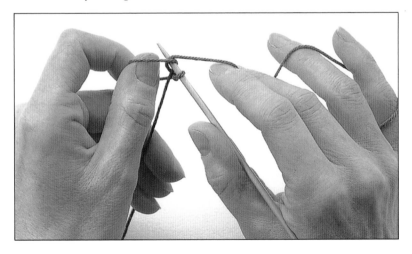

3 Take the yarn around the needle, then draw a loop through to make a stitch. Gently pull the end to close the stitch up

to the needle. Repeat until the required number of stitches, including the slip stitch, have been cast on.

The Knit Stitch

When you've mastered the thumb cast on, you'll find the knit stitch—the most basic of stitches—very familiar.

GARTER STITCH

If you knit every stitch of every row, the result is garter stitch. Although it's simple, this reversible fabric can be very versatile. Knitted loosely, it's soft and springy.

Worked firmly, the fabric lies flat, which makes it useful for bands and borders. Garter stitch makes an elastic fabric in which the stitches are stretched widthwise, while the rows draw up to give an almost square gauge.

MAKING A KNIT STITCH

Choose to hold the yarn and needles in whichever way you feel most comfortable.

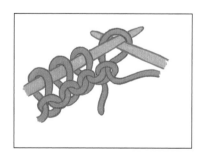

1 Insert the right needle into the first stitch on the left needle. Make sure it goes from left to right into the front of the stitch.

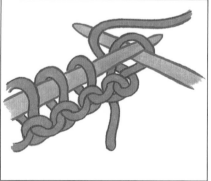

2 Taking the yarn behind, bring it up and around the right needle.

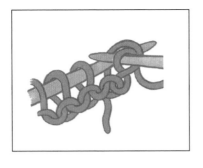

3 Using the tip of the right needle, draw a loop of yarn through the stitch.

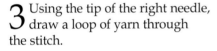

4 Slip the stitch off the left needle. There is now a new stitch on the right needle.

KNITTING A ROW

Continue making stitches on the right needle until all stitches have been worked off the left needle, then hold the needle with the stitches in your left hand for the next row. You'll soon find that the movements flow into each other as you pick up more speed.

TIP

Learning to knit successfully relies upon training both hands to create a knitted stitch. If you are left-handed, try to follow the same instructions as for right-handed people. Reversing the process can create problems when working from charts and patterns.

The Purl Stitch

To progress to stockinette and more stitch patterns, you'll need to know how to purl. Purling isn't difficult—just think of it as the opposite of a knit stitch.

MAKING A PURL STITCH

Hold the yarn and needles in the same way as for making a knit stitch.

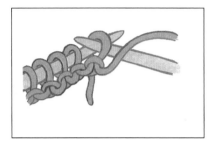

1 Insert the right needle into the first stitch on the left needle. Make sure it goes into the stitch from right to left.

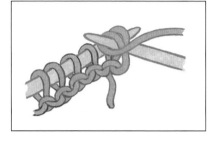

2 Taking the yarn to the front, loop it around the right needle.

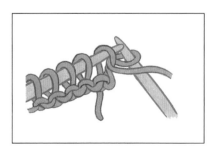

3 Lower the tip of the right needle, taking it away from you to draw a loop of yarn through the stitch.

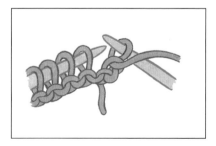

4 Slip the stitch off the left needle. There is now a new stitch on the right needle.

STOCKINETTE STITCH

The best known combination of knit and purl is called stockinette stitch. It's very simple—just knit one row and purl one row alternately.

TIPS
FOR PROFESSIONAL RESULTS

• A less robust cast on is made if you take the needle into the stitch instead of between stitches. The edge is useful for hems.

• To count rows in stockinette stitch, count the ridges on the reverse. For garter stitch, count each ridge as two rows.

• BASIC SKILLS •

REVERSE STOCKINETTE STITCH

The right side of a stockinette is smooth and the other side is ridged. If you use the ridged side of the piece, it is called reverse stockinette.

29

Casting Off

Casting off—also called binding off—links stitches to make a neat edge that won't unravel.

Although there's one basic method of casting off, there are simple variations that can be useful. Chain cast off is the easiest and most used. The decrease cast off is less well known, but gives a very smooth finish. Casting off with a crochet hook makes it easy to cope with slippery yarns or tight stitches.

These diagrams show casting off on the right side of stockinette; however, you can cast off on a wrong-side row or in knit and purl, depending on the stitch pattern.

CHAIN CAST OFF

Lifting one stitch over the next makes a chain along the top of the knitting on the side the cast off is worked.

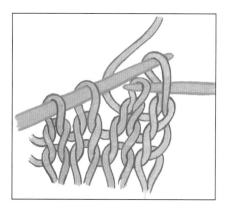
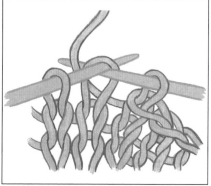

1 Start by knitting the first two stitches. Use the point of the left needle to lift the first of these stitches over the second stitch and off the needle.

2 Knit the next stitch so that there are two stitches on the right needle, then lift the first over the second. Repeat until there is one stitch left. Break the yarn, draw it through the stitch, and pull it tight.

DECREASE CAST OFF

This cast off doesn't make a chain, so it's useful for an edge that is going to be sewn down.

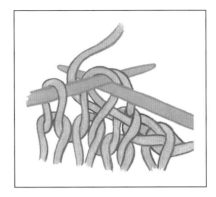

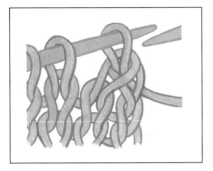

1 Knit the first two stitches together, then slip the stitch just made onto the left needle.

2 Knit together the first two stitches on the left needle, the one already worked and the next one. Slip the stitch just made onto the left needle, as before. Repeat until one stitch is left. Break the yarn, draw it through the stitch, and pull it tight.

CROCHET CAST OFF

This cast off can be as tight or as loose as necessary, according to the tensioning of the crochet chain.

Hold the yarn in your left hand. Slip the first stitch onto the hook. Insert the hook into the next stitch, catch the yarn, and pull it through both stitches. Repeat to the last stitch, break the yarn, and pull it through.

Picking Up Dropped Stitches

Occasionally stitches come off the needle and must be replaced on the needle so that a ladder is not formed. If the stitch has run down only one row or so, the stitch can be re-formed using the needles. But when the stitch has run down several rows, it is easier to pick up the stitch using a crochet hook.

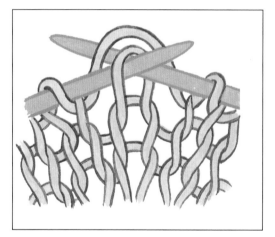

1 If the stitch has dropped one or two rows, lift the strand onto the needle behind the dropped stitch. Use the left needle to take the stitch over the strand, and lift the new stitch back onto the left needle, making sure it faces the correct way.

2 If the stitch has dropped a long way, insert the hook through the dropped stitch from the front, then catch the strand and pull it through to make a new stitch. Put the last stitch on the left needle. Each strand of the ladder is a row, so make sure you catch all of them.

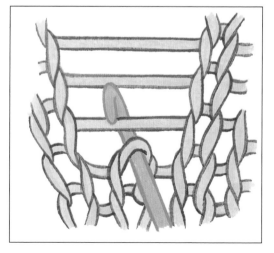

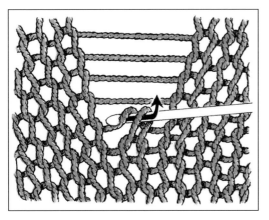

PICKING UP A KNIT STITCH

From the front, insert the crochet hook into the fallen stitch. Catch the first of the horizontal strands with the hook and pull it through the stitch, thus forming a new stitch. Repeat this process for the length of the ladder, placing the last stitch back on the needle.

PICKING UP A PURL STITCH

A purl stitch can be easily picked up from the back of the work, following the procedure for the knit stitches. If you need to pick up from the purl side, insert the crochet hook through the fabric and into the stitch from the front of the stitch or the back of the work. Catch the horizontal strand lying at the front of the work and pull it through the stitch. The stitch will now be twisted, so the hook must be removed from the stitch and reinserted in order to repeat the process up the length of the ladder.

When a section of work is completed, it is necessary to remove the stitches from the needle in a way that will keep the last row of stitches from "running," and forming ladders. This is known as casting or binding off. In most places, the cast-off edge should be firm, but occasionally it needs to be loose. To obtain a loose cast off, the stitches can be worked very loosely or a larger needle can be used. When working with yarns that have a very fine core thread, such as mohair, it is important not to cast off too tightly, as this can ruin the shape of the garment. Usually, the cast-off edge should have the same tension as the rest of the garment, neither pulled in nor splayed out.

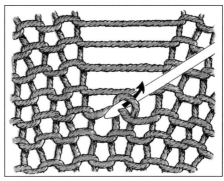

Shapings

Now that you know the basics, you'll want to make something to wear. Here's how to shape your knitting, follow instructions, and sew up your work beautifully.

When shaping your knitting, increases make the fabric wider and decreases make it narrower. Increases and decreases can also be used to create stitch patterns.

Understanding the instructions for the design you've chosen is easy if you take it one step at a time. Charts are a wonderfully clear explanation of stitch patterns and are simple to use once you know how. And you will also discover that the secret of a beautiful garment is knitting to the correct gauge and knowing the best way to sew up for a perfect finish.

SIMPLE SHAPINGS

When knitting, you can shape at the same time as creating the fabric.

One-stitch increases and decreases are used to shape sleeves, armholes, and necks. They can be both practical and decorative. Fully fashioned shapings are made several stitches in from the edges so that the increases and decreases become a feature of the design. Shapings can also be used across a row; for example, stitches may be increased or decreased at the top of a rib.

TIPS
FOR PROFESSIONAL RESULTS

• If your chain cast off is too tight, especially at a neck edge, cast off with a needle one or more sizes larger.

On this fully fashioned shaping (right), the bar increases are made to look as though they are two stitches in from the edge.

Increasing

At various times in the making of a garment, you may need to add stitches to the work, either at the edge or at some point across the row. If you intend to design your own garments, you will need to understand the various methods of increasing so that you can use the correct form of increasing in the correct place.

WORKING TWO STITCHES FROM ONE

On a knit row

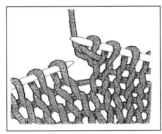

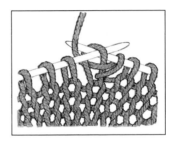

1 This method of increasing causes a knot to form on the left of the worked stitch.

2 Knit the stitch as usual, but do not drop the stitch from the left-hand needle; knit into the back of the same stitch, then remove it from the left-hand needle.

On a purl row

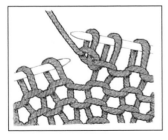

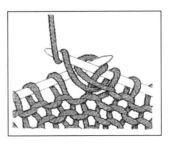

1 A knot is formed to the left of the worked stitch.

2 Purl into the stitch as usual, but do not remove the stitch from the left-hand needle.

RAISED INCREASE

The loop lying between two stitches is raised, twisted, and placed on the needle. (It must be twisted in order to keep a hole from forming.)

On a knit row

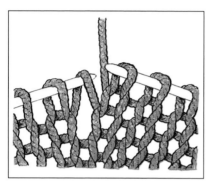

1 Insert tip of left-hand needle under thread running between the stitches, from front to back.

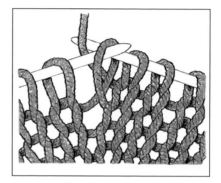

2 Work a knit stitch into the back of this raised stitch.

On a purl row

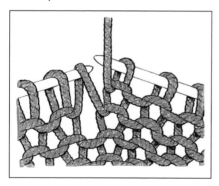

1 Insert tip of left-hand needle under thread running between the stitches, from front to back.

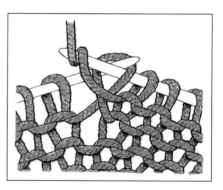

2 Work a purl stitch into the back of this raised stitch.

DECORATIVE INCREASE

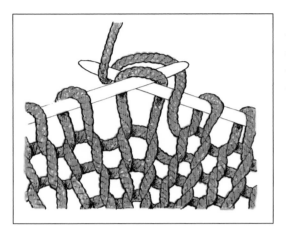

When this increase is worked in, it forms a hole that can be used in a decorative manner.

On a knit row
Bring your yarn to the front of the work, then knit the next stitch as usual (see above), forming a loop over the needle. On the following row, this loop is purled as usual and a hole is formed.

On a purl row
Take the yarn to the back of the work, then purl the next stitch as usual, forming a loop over the needle (see below). On the following row, this stitch is knitted as usual and a hole is formed.

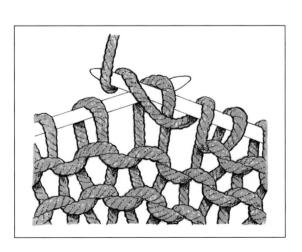

VARIOUS STYLES OF INCREASING

A Increases on a purl row. Working two stitches from one, the increases are worked in the first stitch of the row, then in the last stitch, so that both edges are smooth.

B Increases on a knit row. The right side of this example (which has been worked two stitches from one) has a smooth edge. The left side is "bumpy" when the increases are worked on the first and last stitches of the row.

C & **D** Raised and decorative increases. Both are made at least one stitch in from either edge and look the same at both edges. They are worked on every alternate (or knit) row.

A   **B**   **C**   **D**

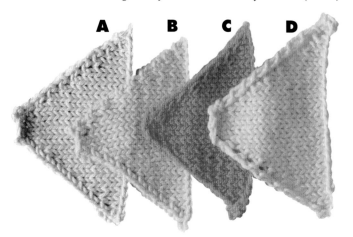

FULLY FASHIONED INCREASE

These are formed by working any of the increases several stitches in from the edge, causing the edge stitches to slant in the direction of the shaping.

E   **F**   **G**

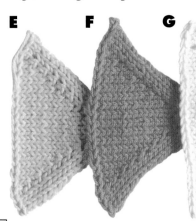

E Working two stitches from one, work in the third stitch from the beginning of the row and the fourth stitch from the end of the row, worked here on every alternate (or knit) row.

F Raised increases are worked here on every alternate (or knit) row, four stitches in from the edge.

G Decorative increases are worked here on every alternate (or knit) row, three stitches from the edge.

Decreasing

Decreases, like increases, have to be worked at various times during the making of a garment in order to achieve the correct shaping.

CAST-OFF DECREASE

This is used where several stitches are to be cast off, either at the edge

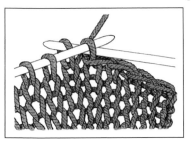

or in the middle of a row. Stitches are not usually cast off at the end of a row, but if this is necessary, the yarn has to be cut and rejoined at the beginning of the next row.

Cast off in the usual manner for the required number of stitches. The last stitch left on the right-hand needle must not be counted as a cast-off stitch.

SIMPLE DECREASE

When the decrease is to be worked at the edge of a piece, and where that edge is to be enclosed within a seam, the easiest way to work this

decrease is to work the two edge stitches together, either knitwise or purlwise.

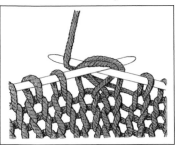

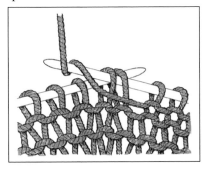

On a knit row
From the front, insert the right-hand needle through the next two stitches. Work them together as a single knit stitch.

On a purl row
From the front, insert the right-hand needle through the next two stitches. Work them together as a single purl stitch.

VISIBLE OR FULLY FASHIONED DECREASE

When decreases are worked, they form a slant, either to the right or to the left. There are two main ways of decreasing:

a) where two stitches are worked together, and

b) when one stitch is passed over another stitch, as in casting off. This is called the slip-stitch decrease. Each of these methods can be worked either on the knit or on the purl side of stocking stitch fabric, and each can be worked to produce a slant to the right or the left. When designing knitted garments, it is important to know each of these variations so that slants to the right or left can be used as part of the design feature. When forming fully fashioned decreases, these visible decreases are used several stitches in from the edge.

KNIT TWO STITCHES TOGETHER

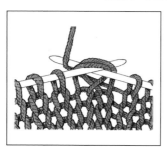

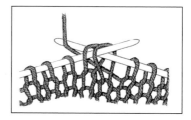

With slant to right on right side of work
Work two sides together knitwise, as for the simple decrease.

With slant to left on right side of work
Slip first two stitches from left needle to right needle separately, knitwise. Replace them both on left needle, then knit them together through back of loops.

PURL TWO STITCHES TOGETHER

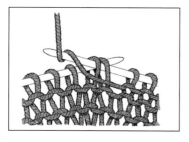

With slant to right on right side of work
Work two stitches together purlwise, as for the simple decrease.

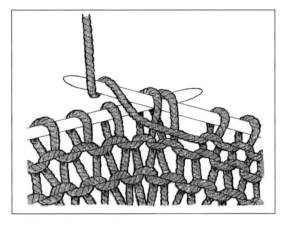

With slant to left on right side of work

Slip first two stitches from left needle to right needle separately, knitwise. Replace them both on the left needle and purl both stitches together through back of loops (insert needle from back of second stitch, through both stitches).

SLIP-STITCH DECREASE WORKED KNITWISE

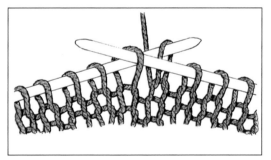

With slant to right on right side of work

Knit one stitch, replace this stitch on left needle, pass next stitch over this stitch, and return the first stitch to the right needle.

With slant to left on right side of work

Slip next stitch onto right needle, knit next stitch, and pass the first stitch over this new stitch, as in casting off.

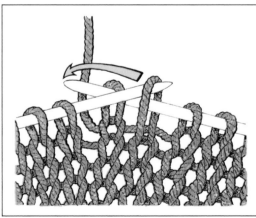

SLIP-STITCH DECREASE WORKED PURLWISE

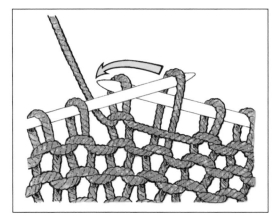

With slant to right on right side of work

Slip next stitch onto right needle, purlwise. Purl next stitch and pass slip stitch over this stitch, as in casting off.

With slant to left on right side of work

Purl one stitch, slip next stitch knitwise, then return it to left needle, return the purled stitch to left needle also, pass the slip stitch over this stitch, and return the stitch to right needle.

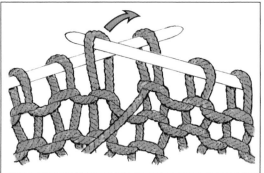

Work the decreases in pairs, using complementary methods. For a smooth line of shapings, work a decrease slanting left near the beginning of the row and a decrease slanting right near the end. For a feathered effect, reverse the decreases.

Normal decrease

Feathered decrease

Picking Up Stitches

The edges of a finished garment are usually neatened by the addition of a band of knitting. This band of knitting also holds the edge firm and keeps the garment in shape. Picking up stitches is not difficult, but it is possible to spoil a well-knitted garment by inattention to detail at this point.

Most bands to be added need to be slightly tighter than the rest of the work in order to keep the garment in shape. This is achieved by any one of the following: using smaller size needles; using a stitch pattern that pulls the work in, e.g., ribbing; using finer yarn and needles; and picking up fewer stitches. Commercial patterns will state how many stitches should be picked up along the edge. Don't be afraid to change the number of stitches if you are not happy with the result.

HOW TO PICK UP A STITCH

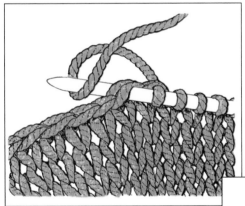

1 With one needle in the right hand, insert tip through edge of work from the right side, pass end of yarn around needle, and, taking care not to lose this stitch, pull it through to the front. The stitches shown here are being picked up from a horizontal section of work.

2 The stitches shown here are picked up along a vertical section of work.

43

POINTS
TO REMEMBER

• Pick up stitches at least one stitch in from the edge (or the approximate width of one stitch). Never pick up stitches right on the edge.

• When working along a straight horizontal or vertical edge, pick up all the stitches along the same line or row of stitches.

• Avoid picking up stitches into loose or baggy stitches.

• When working along a vertical edge, pick up one stitch for every row except every third or fourth row.

• The stitches should be picked up evenly along the edge. To achieve this, divide the work into sections, marking each section with a pin. Divide the total number of stitches into the same number of sections, then pick up the correct number of stitches within each section.

CURVES AND CORNERS

Although the band must be shaped if it is to have a corner, the stitches are picked up evenly as given for a straight edge. Curves must be treated differently.

• Where the work is convex, slightly more stitches should be picked up. When casting off a band on a convex curve, it is a good idea to cast off slightly looser than for the rest of the work.

• Where the work is concave, slightly fewer stitches should be picked up. When casting off a band on a concave curve, cast off slightly tighter than for the rest of the work.

PICKING UP STITCHES FROM THE MIDDLE OF A PIECE OF WORK

Sometimes it is necessary to pick up stitches across the center of the fabric. First tack a line where the stitches are to be picked up, then pick up stitches as for the edge, but insert the needle through the fabric. Make sure that the stitches are always picked up from the same line or row of stitches and from the same section of each stitch.

Buttons and Buttonholes

The overall appearance of a garment is largely determined by the way it closes, so you should think about how you're going to fasten a garment early on in the design process. Buttons tend to be the most popular of all fastenings, since they are generally lightweight, easy to attach, and do not stretch the knitted fabric.

If you are working from an existing knitting pattern, you can select the buttons once the piece is finished. However, if you have specific buttons that you wish to use, then it is wise to think about the size and shape of the buttonhole in advance.

Make sure that the button is not too heavy or bulky and will not stretch the garment or catch on the yarn. It is a good idea to buy an extra button and sew it to the inside of the side seam in case it is needed for repairs.

TIPS
FOR PROFESSIONAL RESULTS

• To pick up a given number of stitches along an edge, fold it in half, mark the halfway point, then fold each half and mark the quarters. Divide the number of stitches by four and pick up this number of stitches evenly from each marked corner.

CHOOSING BUTTONS

Buttons are made in a variety of materials, from wood, bone, and mother-of-pearl to gold, silver, and copper. Mass-produced buttons are made from plastic and glass. Most buttons come with either two or four holes through the center, or with a shank made from a metal loop.

"Natural" buttons such as horn or wood work well on traditionally styled knitwear such as Aran. Fancy buttons, such as gold or diamante, are more suited to cotton and silk. The other thing to consider when choosing a button is the size of the buttonhole. This depends primarily on the type of yarn used and the style of garment. A garment knitted in chunky yarn requires a large button—preferably one with a shank—and therefore needs a large buttonhole. A buttonhole for a flat, sewn-through button is smaller than the one for a raised button.

HOW TO SEW A BUTTON IN PLACE

If a button is not attached to the knitted piece correctly, it can pull and stretch the fabric. If the garment has been worked in a lightweight yarn such as a 4-ply, then you can use the same yarn to attach a button. For thicker, chunkier knits, use a sewing thread of the same color.

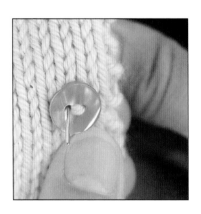

1 Use a long length of yarn, knotted at one end, and a sharp sewing needle. Sew the button in place either through the holes or the shank, depending on the type of button selected.

2 Once the button is secure, wrap the yarn around the sewn stitches between the button and the garment at least three times. Secure the yarn on the reverse of the fabric.

HOW TO MAKE BUTTONS

In some cases, you may not be able to find a button that is suitable for your garment. Making the button, as well as the knitted piece, will create a truly original and personal project.

Dorset buttons

Dorset buttons can be made in almost endless permutations of color or just one color. Dorset buttons are especially effective on cushions and garments that require larger buttons, since small ones can be tricky to make.

1 Using a long length of yarn, sew around the edge of a small curtain ring using buttonhole or blanket stitch. Holding the tail end of the yarn close to the ring, sew around both the ring and the tail until it has disappeared. Secure once the ring is full and turn the hem edge of the blanket stitch to the inside of the ring.

2 Using a second yarn, sew around the ring to create a web effect. Using two or three stitches, oversew the center of the spokes and secure the yarn.

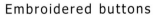

3 Using a third yarn, thread the needle through from the back to the front of the button, close to the center of the web, between two spokes. Fill in the ring's center by working backstitch around the spokes. Fasten off the yarn.

Embroidered buttons

You can buy button kits that consist of a two-part button: One side acts as the front and the other side has a slot that holds the shank in place.

Fabric is placed over the front of the button and then clipped into place with the secured piece.

Knitted bobble

A knitted bobble, or round ball, can be used as a substitute for a button, provided it is made of a fairly substantial yarn. Bobbles look effective on Aran or cable designs and can be used with a loop fastening. It is a good idea to use a knitting needle smaller than the one used to knit the piece.

Cast on three stitches. Knit one row. Next row: Increase into first stitch, k1, then increase into the last stitch. Turn and knit to end. Continue to increase in this way on every alternate row to the required number of stitches. (The more stitches, the larger the bobble.) Work one row. Decrease the stitches by knitting 2tog tbl. Knit to last two stitches, k2tog. Work one row. Continue to decrease in this way on every alternate row until three stitches are left. Bind off. Stitch running stitch around the edge and pull up the thread to form a bobble. Secure ends of yarn and sew bobble in place.

BUTTONHOLES

Knitting forms a very elastic fabric; if worked incorrectly, buttonholes can look unsightly.

Buy the buttons before working the buttonholes so that the correct size of buttonhole can be worked. Because of the elasticity of the knitted fabric, the buttonhole needs to be smaller than the diameter of the button to keep the buttons fastened. However, if the buttonhole is too large, it can be partially sewn up without looking too unsightly, whereas if the buttonhole is too small there is very little that can be done about it other than changing the buttons or reknitting the buttonhole.

SIMPLE EYELET BUTTONHOLE

This forms a very small buttonhole, although the size of a hole varies with the tension of the knitting.

The buttonhole is worked over two stitches by bringing yarn to the front of the work, then knitting two stitches together. On the following row, the yarn over the stitch should be worked as a normal stitch.

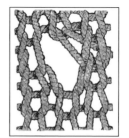

HORIZONTAL BUTTONHOLE

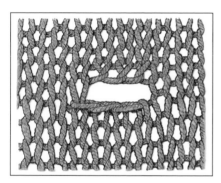

Worked over two rows

Work in pattern to the position of the buttonhole, cast off the required number of stitches, then continue in pattern to the end of the row. On the next row, work in pattern to the cast-off stitches, cast on the same number of stitches as those cast off, then continue in pattern to the end of the row.

Worked over one row

Work in pattern to the position of the buttonhole, bring yarn forward, slip the next stitch, take yarn back, slip the next stitch, pass the first slip stitch over the second, slip the next stitch, pass the second slip stitch over the third slip stitch, and continue to cast off for the required number of stitches. Slip the last stitch back onto the left needle, turn the work, and take the yarn to the back. Then cast on the same number of stitches as those cast off, using the firm knit stitch cast on. Cast on one extra stitch, and, before placing it on the left needle, bring the yarn

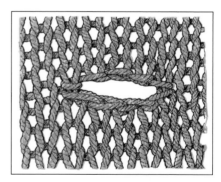

forward, then place it on the left needle. Turn work, slip the next stitch, and pass the last cast-on stitch over this slip stitch. Now continue in pattern across the row.

Tassels

Tassels can look very effective when sewn to the corners of cushions or placed on the ends of knitted cords.

Simple tassels are very easy to make and can add a unique finishing touch to the knitted piece. Tassels can use up a lot of yarn, so make sure that you have plenty and make them after the knitted piece is complete.

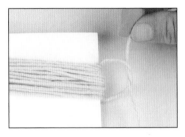

1 Wrap the yarn around a piece of cardboard that is the same length as the tassel.

2 Thread a second piece of yarn through the top end of the tassel between the yarn and the cardboard and tie to secure, leaving a long end of yarn to tie around the tassel.

3 Cut along the yarn at the bottom edge and remove the cardboard. Thread the long end through a knitter's sewing needle and down through the center of the tassel from the top.

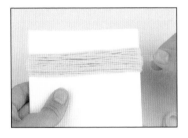

4 Wrap the yarn around the tassel as many times as required. Thread the needle through to the top of the tassel and trim.

Pom-poms

Pom-pom making is a very popular pastime for small children and is a fantastic way to introduce them to yarns and the concept of knitting.

Pom-poms can look lovely hanging from shelves or a Christmas tree and are particularly effective on cushions and winter hats. You can buy a pom-pom maker, but circles of cardboard work just as well. Cut two circles bigger than the required diameter of the pom-pom, with a smaller hole at the center.

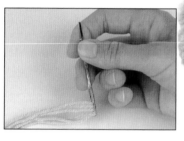

1 Thread a large sewing needle or bodkin with as many ends of yarn as it will take. The yarn ends should be approximately 3 ft. long.

2 Hold the two circles together and thread the needle through the center, around the outside, and back through the center from the front, holding the tail end of yarn in place with your thumb if needed. Continue to do this until the central hole is full.

3 Using a sharp pair of scissors, cut around the pom-pom, between the two circles.

4 Tie a piece of yarn or sewing thread around the center of the pom-pom as tightly as possible and remove the circles. Trim the pom-pom to form a ball.

Tension

It cannot be overemphasized that a garment may be drastically altered in shape and size if you do not make sure that you have the correct tension.

Knitting patterns are written by means of mathematical calculations based on two sets of figures, the first being the size of the piece of work required in centimeters, the second being the number of stitches and rows required to knit each centimeter. This is called the tension. Tension is affected by thickness of yarn, size of needles, the flow of yarn that is controlled by the knitter, and the stitch pattern. In theory, it would be possible to knit any thickness of yarn using any size of needle. However, a chunky yarn knitted on very small needles would both look and feel like cardboard, while a fine yarn knitted on large needles would produce a fabric that was too loose to be of any use. There is obviously a happy medium, where the fabric both looks and feels good and is also elastic and firm. Each yarn has a tension recommended by the manufacturer, some of whom display this information on the ball band label.

Individual knitters vary in tension, so sometimes, to achieve the correct tension, it is necessary to change to larger or smaller needles than those recommended. Recommended needle sizes are often given on the ball band as well.

Having obtained the correct tension over stocking stitch, the remaining factor that influences tension is the stitch pattern. Textured or Fair Isle stitch patterns often pull the work in so that more stitches are needed, whereas lace patterns often need fewer stitches,

TIP
FOR A PROFESSIONAL RESULT

• The ball band often gives the manufacturer's recommended stockinette gauge, but you should always check your gauge in the stitch pattern as well.

as they are very open. Unless otherwise stated, the tension square should always be worked over the stitch pattern used for the main part of the garment. Once you have worked a fairly large area of the garment, check the tension over part of the knitting, as tension sometimes changes during the knitting, either because the knitter relaxes or because a larger number of stitches affects the way the yarn and needles are held.

HOW TO MEASURE GAUGE

Knit a swatch with the size needles given in the instructions. Always add a few extra stitches and work a few more rows because the edge stitches will be distorted. Check the making-up instructions, and, if necessary, press your swatch. Measure the gauge on a flat surface.

MEASURING STITCHES

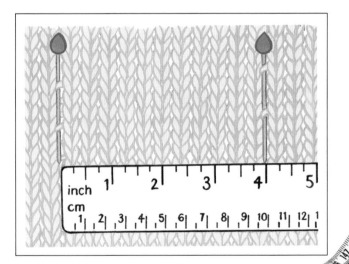

1 Count and mark the stitches with pins, then measure between the pins. If the measurement is correct, you'll know that your finished garment will be the right width. If your marked stitches measure less, you're knitting too tightly and the garment will be too narrow. Knit another swatch

using larger needles and measure again. If the marked stitches measure more than they should, you're knitting loosely and the garment will be too wide. Knit another swatch on smaller needles and measure again.

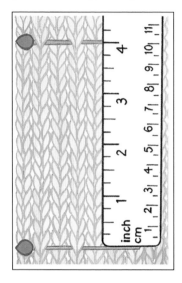

2 Mark the number of rows and check the measurement. If it's correct, go ahead and start knitting. If the marked rows measure less, your knitting is tight and the garment will be too short. Try using larger needles for your next swatch. If the marked rows measure more, your knitting is loose and the garment will be too long. Try knitting another swatch using smaller needles.

HOW NEEDLE SIZE AFFECTS GAUGE

See how the same yarn, the same number of stitches, and the same number of rows worked by the same knitter give different-size swatches depending on the size of the needles.

TIPS
FOR PROFESSIONAL RESULTS

• Use a tape measure to make sure you have the correct gauge.

• Use pins to mark the distance between stitches.

Small needles

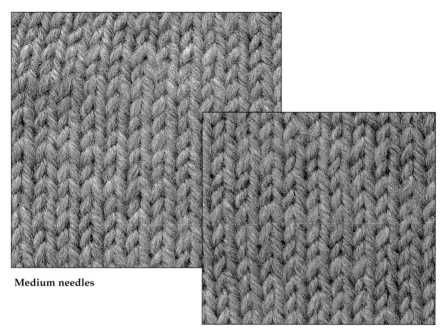

Medium needles

Large needles

TIP
FOR A PROFESSIONAL RESULT

• When joining in new yarn, start a
new ball of yarn at the beginning of
a row, where the edge will be part of
a seam. Make a neat bundle with the
tail end of yarn left from the old ball.
To join the new yarn, make a single
overhand knot. When sewing up,
undo the knot, thread one end
onto a sewing needle, and run it
through a few stitches of the seam.

Reading Patterns and Charts

Reading a knitting pattern may be unfamiliar at first, but as soon as you've cracked the code, you'll be able to follow instructions with confidence.

WHAT ARE THE MEASUREMENTS?

The sizes will be set out in sequence, as a grid or with larger sizes in brackets. Because fit varies so much from one design to another, first compare the actual bust or chest measurement with your body measurement, then check the length and sleeves. Some garments are designed to fit closely, while others are very loose—choose the fit you want.

WHAT DO YOU NEED TO BUY?

It's important to buy the yarn specified. Another yarn, however similar, may not behave in the same way and you might need a different amount. Make sure you buy enough yarn—and make sure that you have everything else listed.

CHECKING YOUR GAUGE

Gauge is given as the number of stitches and rows, usually 4 in. over the stitch pattern on the recommended-size needles. The needle size should be treated as a guide only—you may need to use a different size to knit to the gauge given in the instructions.

SIZES

Patterns are usually designed for several sizes and the instructions for each consecutive size are written in brackets. For example, cast on 12 (14; 16; 18; 20) sts, and knit for 0.8 (0.9; 1.3) in.

To prevent confusion, after choosing your size, encircle each of the relevant instructions before starting to knit.

ASTERISKS

These are used to show where a piece of work is to be repeated. Groups of asterisks may be used

---

TIP
FOR A PROFESSIONAL RESULT

• Enlarging a chart by photocopying can make it easier to follow. Make several copies and glue or tape them together. If it helps, draw any shapings on the photocopy.

---

to repeat different sections of the work. For example: k2 (3; 3; 4; 5) sts ** k4 *p2, k2 rep from * once more. K2 rep from ** 4 more times. In this example, all the work from the double asterisks has to be repeated four more times, and the single asterisks once, within each of the repeats. Brackets are used sometimes in place of asterisks.

REVERSING SHAPINGS AND PATTERNS

Sometimes the instructions for one side of a garment are given and for the other side the instructions will state that you should work the same as the first side, "reversing shapings" (and sometimes the stitch or color pattern). This usually only happens in simple patterns. Where the pattern is more complex, it may be easier to work out and write down specific instructions, using the first side as a guide.

MATERIALS

All patterns state the amount of yarn required but as this can only be an approximation, it is a good idea to buy an extra ball or make sure that you will be able to get extra yarn in the same color and dye lot if necessary.

CHARTS AND GRAPHS

These sometimes appear instead of written instructions for a stitch or color pattern.

Color knitting charts

Most color knitting is in stockinette, so every right side row is knit and every wrong side row is purl, with the squares on the chart showing the color to be used. The chart may be printed in color or may use a symbol for each color. If any textured stitches are used, they will be shown as symbols and explained in the key.

Reading charts

Every stitch and every row is shown as on the right side of the knitting. A blank square represents knit on a right side row and purl on a wrong side row — making stockinette. A dot represents purl on a right side row and knit on a wrong side row — making reverse stockinette.

Some symbols represent more than one stitch, such as a decrease. Where the stitch count varies within a stitch pattern, solid areas compensate for the missing stitches. Not all methods of charting use the same symbols, so always check the key.

Abbreviations

The following abbreviations are commonly found in knitting patterns. Abbreviations are used to save space and make written patterns easier to follow. Some pattern writers use slightly different abbreviations, but in most cases, there will be a list of abbreviations at some stage of the pattern.

alt	alternate
beg	beginning
bo	bind off
cm	centimeter
cn	cable needle
co	cast on
cont	continue
dec	decrease
dk	double knitting
dpn	double-pointed needle
foll	following
fwd	forward
G st	garter stitch
in.	inches
inc	increase
incl	including
k	knit
kwise	knitwise
mb	make bobble
mm	millimeter
m1	make one stitch
no	number
oz	ounce
p	purl
patt	pattern

pfb	purl into the front and the back of the stitch
pnso	pass next stitch over
psso	pass slip stitch over
ptbl	pass through back loop
p2tog	purl two together
pwise	purlwise
rem	remaining
rep	repeat
rev St st	reverse stockinette stitch
rh	right hand
sl	slip
sk	skip
skp	slip 1 stitch, knit 1 stitch, pass slip stitch over
ssk	slip slip knit
st	stitch
St st	stockinette stitch
tbl	through back loop
tog	together
ws	wrong side
wyb	with yarn in back
wyf	with yarn in front
ybk	yarn back
yfon	yarn forward and over needle
yfrn	yarn forward and round needle
yfwd	yarn forward
yo	yarn over
yo twice or **yo2**	yarn over needle twice
yon	yarn over needle
yrn	yarn round needle

Using Sets of Needles

This is the most common method of producing tubular fabric for socks, stockings, sleeves, etc.

The needles are double-pointed so that the work can be knitted from either end. They are usually sold in sets of four needles and are available in several lengths. They can be used in more or less quantity, although knitting with six is usually the maximum. The number of stitches required is divided between the needles, leaving one needle free to knit with.

Cast the required number of stitches onto each needle. Draw the first of these cast-on stitches close to the last cast-on stitch. Using the spare needle, knit the first cast-on stitch, thus closing the "circle." Then continue to knit to the last of the stitches on the first needle. All the stitches are now transferred to the spare needle and the first needle is now the spare needle. Continue to knit from the next needle, using this spare needle. Continue working in this manner to the end of the row (or round). Mark the first or the last stitch of the round with a colored thread and move it up every time a row is completed as it is very easy to get lost and not know the beginning from the end.

When knitting a tubular fabric, it is not necessary to work any purl rows in order to obtain stocking

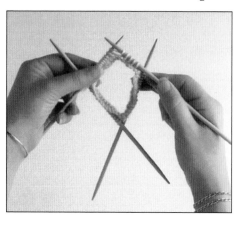

Knitting with four needles

stitch, as all the rows are worked from the front, or knit side, of the fabric. To obtain garter stitch, knit and purl rows must be alternated (as for stocking stitch worked on two needles). Obviously, stitch patterns for tubular fabric must be written differently and some patterns cannot be adapted from two needles to tubular fabric, and vice versa.

If you have trouble keeping the stitches on the needles, a cork or something similar can be stuck onto the ends of the needles.

USING CIRCULAR KNITTING NEEDLES

These usually come in the following lengths: 15½ in., 23½ in., 31 in., and 39 in. They can be used instead of pairs or sets of needles. Some advantages of using a circular needle are

Knitting with circular needles

that they can accommodate more stitches, there is no possibility of losing one of the needles, the stitches cannot fall off the ends, and they are less cumbersome.

When working in place of two needles, any length of circular needle can be used. With one end of the needle in each hand, cast on the required number in each hand and cast on the required number of stitches. Begin knitting, starting by working into the last cast-on stitch and then continuing to transfer all the stitches from the left-hand needle to the right-hand needle in the usual manner. When the last stitch has been worked, change hands so that the last stitch worked is now at the end of the needle in your left hand. Knit this last stitch using the right-hand needle and continue in this manner, changing hands every time a row is complete.

The length of needle to be used in place of sets of needles depends on the number of stitches to be cast on. They must be able to be evenly spaced from end to end without being stretched. One may need to change to a different length of needle during the working of a garment if the shaping causes the number of stitches to decrease.

The required number of stitches should be cast on, then the circle is closed by changing hands and working into the first of the cast-on stitches. Continue knitting in rounds without changing hands.

• BASIC SKILLS •

TIP
FOR A PROFESSIONAL RESULT

• If a plastic circular needle is stiff and curly after storage, soak it in warm water for a few minutes, then straighten it between your fingers.

Partial Knitting

Garments can be given shape not only by means of increases and decreases but also by means of partial knitting.

Areas of garments can be partially knitted so that one edge of the work is longer than the other edge, and by this means shaping can be created to form darts, shoulder seams, yoke shapings, and collars.

In order to prevent the formation of holes when turning the work, wrap the yarn around the first of the stitches to be left unworked before continuing to knit on the remaining stitches.

PARTIAL KNITTING

The sample shown here was worked over twenty-one stitches and the outside edge became twice as long as the inside edge.

1st row: knit.
2nd row: purl.
3rd row: knit to last 7 sts, yf, sl1, yb, return sl st to LN, turn work.
4th row: purl these 14 sts.
5th row: knit all the sts.
6th row: purl all the sts.
7th row: knit to last 14 sts, yf, sl1, yb, return sl st to LN, turn work.
8th row: purl these 7 sts.
Rep from row 1 as necessary.

WORKING INTO THE BACK OF A STITCH

The knit and purl stitches are normally formed by working into the front loops of the stitches on the left needle but they can also be worked by knitting into the back loops. When this is done, the resulting dropped stitch is twisted if all the stitches of stocking stitch fabric are worked into the back of the loop (on both the knit and the purl rows). The result will be a very twisted fabric with little elasticity. However, if the stitches are knitted into the back of the loop on either the knit or the purl row but not on both, the resulting fabric will have a slightly twisted stitch effect called continental stocking stitch.

Partial knitting

Continental stocking stitch

Making Up

Assembling a knitted garment involves two processes—pressing each piece of knitting, then sewing them together.

PRESSING

Pinning out and pressing your knitting before sewing up will make an enormous difference to the finished garment. Always check the ball band for yarn care and test a sample swatch before applying heat or steam to your knitting—natural fiber yarns are usually quite robust, but man-made mixes can collapse and therefore need a cool, dry iron. Pin each piece out to size with the right side down on a padded board, using a tape measure to check the measurement. Then lay a dampened cotton muslin cloth on top and gently apply the iron. Remember never to stamp the iron down or push it along the surface of the knitting.

If the yarn is delicate or if the stitch pattern is textured, pin out the pieces but do not press. Instead, dampen them with a water spray, then leave them to dry naturally.

SEWING UP

Sewing up from the right side is the secret of invisible seams. This method, also known as ladder or mattress stitch, is good for joining side and sleeve seams in most stitch patterns.

INVISIBLE SEAM

Place both pieces of knitting flat, with right sides facing and the edges to be joined running

vertically. Thread a wool needle with yarn and secure at one lower edge—the first side. Take the needle under the cast-on edge of the second side, draw the yarn through, then go under the first cast-on edge again. Tension the yarn to level the edges. Take the needle under the strand between the edge stitch and the next stitch on the first row of the second side and draw the yarn through. Repeat for the first row of the first side. Continue joining row ends from alternate sides in this way, without splitting stitches.

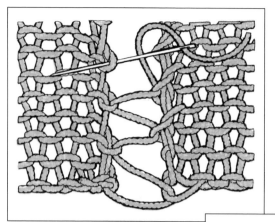

1 Place the edges next to each other, rows matching each other, row for row. Sew in a zigzag fashion through the knot of each row, alternating from edge to edge, then pull the work together so that it is firmly held but not too tight.

2 The finished edge-to-edge seam.

BACKSTITCH SEAM

This is the most commonly used form of seam. Strong and firm, it looks neat on the right side of the work. The edges should be

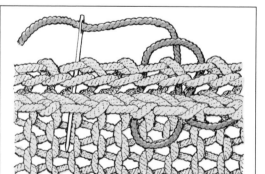

placed next to each other, with right sides facing. Ordinary backstitch is worked along the seam, at least 0.2 in. in from the edge.

1 Work through the center of each stitch to match with the same stitch on the other edge. Work in straight lines through the center of the same line or row of stitches throughout.

2 The finished backstitch seam, shown from the back of the knitting.

RIB
Ribbing needs to be planned so that when the seam is joined, the stitches at each edge combine to make a whole rib.

STRIPES
Stripes and color patterns are easier to match when sewn together from the right side.

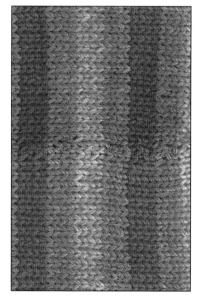

TIP
FOR A PROFESSIONAL RESULT

• Cover your padded ironing board with a checkered fabric to help you line up the rows and stitches when pinning out.

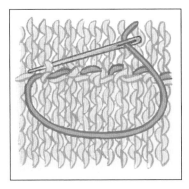

BACKSTITCH

Backstitch makes strong seams. Hold the pieces with right sides together. Thread a wool needle and secure the yarn at the right-hand end. Lining up rows and working one stitch in from the edge, bring the needle up through both pieces of knitting between stitches of first and second rows, then down, between the first row and the cast-on edge. Come up again one or two rows on and go down next to the previous stitch. Complete the seam

SLIP STITCH

Catching down pocket linings or zipper facings is easy with slip stitch. With wrong sides facing, tack the pieces to be joined, matching rows. Thread a wool needle with yarn. Secure the end, then take the needle alternately under a strand on the main fabric and an edge strand. Don't let the stitches show on the right side or pull the yarn too tight.

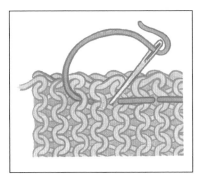

in this way, taking care to work between the knitted stitches.

TIPS
FOR PROFESSIONAL RESULTS

• Always sew in good light. If you are using a dark yarn or if the light is poor, thread a contrasting yarn through the stitches to be sewn together to make them easier to see.

• Use a new piece of yarn, not one that is already attached to the piece. Make sure the yarn is not too long, since this can cause friction while it is being threaded through the knitted piece, which can cause it to break.

Additional Casting On and Off

The basic skills will take you a long way in knitting, but sometimes more unusual techniques can make all the difference. Learning how and when to use these alternatives is the first step toward designing for yourself.

Interesting cast-on or cast-off edgings can transform a simple garment. Tailored effects such as hems and facings give a sophisticated look to knitting and are often the best solution when planning borders for color or intarsia knitting. Grafting is a useful emergency technique for changing the length of a piece of knitting and can be adapted to make almost invisible seams. Turning rows are a subtle way to shape within the fabric of the knitting, while adding more increases and decreases to your knitting knowledge will help make perfect shapings and more elaborate stitch patterns.

CHANNEL ISLAND CAST ON

Strongly defined knots decorate the edge of this robust cast on. For an odd number of stitches, work as given here. For an even number of stitches, simply cast on one more stitch at the end.

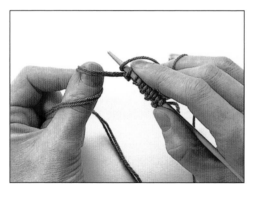

Leaving an end six times the length of the edge to be cast on, put a slipknot on one needle. Double this length back on itself so that the free end hangs down where it meets the needle at the slipknot. Take the doubled end in your left hand and the single strand from the ball in your right hand. Wind the doubled end twice around the thumb of your left hand, insert the needle up and under both of the double strands of yarn on your thumb, and take the single strand around the needle to make a stitch. Pull on the ends to bring the knot up the needle. Bring the single strand forward and over the needle to make a stitch. Continue to make pairs of stitches in this way, ending with a stitch knitted from the thumb.

The decorative quality of this cast on can be seen on the lower edge of a typical Guernsey-style sweater.

KNOTTED CAST ON

Casting on by this method makes a small knot at the base of each stitch and gives an attractive, double-strength edge.

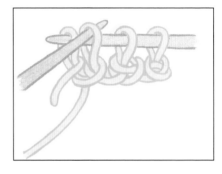

Leaving an end about four times the length of the edge to be cast on, make a slipknot on one needle. Cast on one stitch by the thumb method, then lift the slipknot over the stitch. Cast on two more stitches and take the first of the two over the second for each cast-on stitch required.

PICOT CAST OFF

Instead of a plain cast off, try this very pretty finish. The picots can be made on every stitch, in which case the edge will flute, or they can be spaced with as many chain cast-off stitches between as are needed to make the edge lie flat.

Insert the right needle into the first stitch on the left needle and knit a stitch but do not slip the stitch off the left needle. Slip the new stitch onto the left needle, then make a second new stitch as before. Cast off four stitches, then slip the remaining stitch back onto the left needle. Repeat along the row, making two stitches and casting off four each time.

CAST-OFF SEAMS

Instead of joining back and front shoulder edges by casting them off separately and sewing them together, a softer join is made if the two sets of stitches are cast off together. This can be done invisibly on the wrong side, as shown here, or made into a feature by being cast off with the wrong sides together.

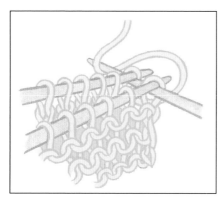

1 Do not cast off the shoulder stitches, but leave them on spare needles. Place the back and front shoulders together with right sides facing and needles pointing in the same direction. Using a third needle, knit the first stitch on the near needle together with the first stitch on the back needle.

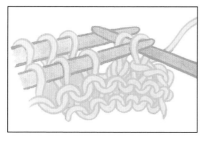

2 Knit the next pair of stitches together and then take the first stitch on the right needle over the second in the usual way. Continue until all the stitches have been cast off. When casting off two pieces of knitting with wrong sides together, make sure that the chain edge of the cast off faces the same way on each shoulder.

TIP
FOR A PROFESSIONAL RESULT

• If you want to join shaped shoulder seams in this way, don't cast off groups of stitches, but work turning rows instead. The shoulders can then be cast off together.

Ribs, Hems, and Facings

As well as making edgings in rib or garter stitch, you can make hems or facings for a more substantial double-fabric finish.

RIBBING

When the knit and purl stitches are alternated not only in rows but also across the stitches of each row, forming vertical lines of alternate knit and purl stitches, it is called ribbing. Alternating the stitches in this way gives the fabric a great deal of elasticity. Because of this, ribbing is often used at the hem or wrist of a garment or wherever it needs to fit well. Ribbing can be worked in a variety of combinations of groups of knit and purl stitches.

When working a purl stitch after a knit stitch, the yarn should be brought to the front of the work prior to working the purl stitch, and when working a knit stitch after a purl stitch, the yarn should be taken to the back of the work before working the knit stitch.

SINGLE RIB

(also called 1x1 rib)
Cast on odd number of stitches.
1st row: *k1, p1, rep from * to the last st, k1.
2nd row: p1, k1, rep from * to the last st, p1.
These two rows should be repeated in the same sequence until the work

measures the correct depth.

As you knit you will find that the fabric pulls in so that only the knit stitches are visible and the purl stitches are hidden.

DOUBLE RIB

(also called 2x2 rib)
Cast on a number of stitches divisible by 4, with 2 extra stitches at the end.
1st row: *k2, p2, rep from * to last 2 sts, k2.

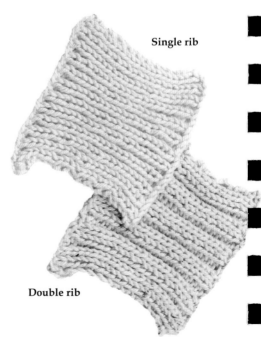

Single rib

Double rib

2nd row: *p2, k2, rep from * to last 2 sts, p2.

Repeat these two rows to the required depth.

The two extra stitches are added in order to centralize the pattern so that it is the same at both edges.

Ribbings can also be worked in a variety of other combinations, such as 3x4, 2x1, and 5x3.

Instead of making edgings in rib or garter stitch, you can make hems or facings for a more substantial double-fabric finish.

MITERED CORNERS

Where a hem or a facing meet, or between an edging and a front band, a mitered corner may be the neatest solution. For this you need to increase one decrease to make a forty-five-degree angle. Shaping on alternate rows in garter stitch or moss stitch produces this angle almost perfectly. In stockinette, achieving the correct angle may entail shaping on a mixture of alternate rows and every row, because the stitches are wider than they are tall.

Here, the garter-stitch edging and front band form a neatly mitered corner.

HEMS

The lower edges of a knitted garment are usually worked ribwise, but sometimes they are "turned up," as in dressmaking. When this kind of hem is worked, care should be taken that it does not curl up. To prevent this it should be partly or wholly worked using smaller needles or fewer stitches.

It is also important that the depth of the hem on the wrong side should be fractionally shorter than the depth of the hem on the right side. This helps to prevent the edge from curling. The fold line of the hem is usually marked in one of two ways.
• Using a row of purl stitches on the right side of the work.

• Knitting the fold row using a needle two or three sizes larger than for the rest of the hem.

Hems can either be sewn or knitted up to finish them.

PLAIN HEM

A knitted hem can be turned up and slip stitched in the same way as a woven fabric hem. This can be bulky and the folded edge may spread, so it's preferable to make a neat, knitted-in hem.

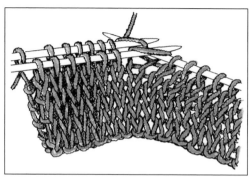

With smaller needles than for the main fabric, cast on fairly loosely using the loop method. Work the depth of the hem in stockinette stitch. Mark the fold with a ridge by working a row out of sequence—either three purl rows or three knit rows, the center row of the three making the ridge. Change to the needles for the main fabric and continue in stockinette stitch until the depth from the ridge matches that of the hem, ending with a purl row. To join the hem on the next row, fold the hem up behind the main fabric, then knit together the first stitch from the left needle with the first stitch from the cast-on edge. Continue in this way to the end of the row.

PICOT HEM

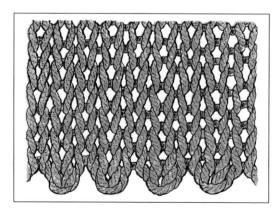

A very attractive way to mark the fold of a hem is to work a row of eyelets that, when the hem is turned up, makes a row of well-defined picots. Work to the depth of the hem, ending with a wrong-side row. If the work contains an odd number of stitches,

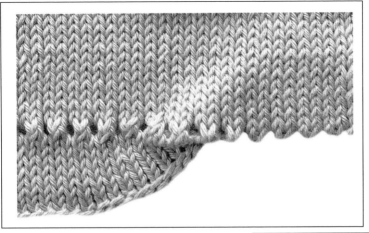

The stitches between the eyelets form the picots when the hem is turned up.

work the next row: k1, *yo, k2tog; rep from * to end. Over an even number of stitches, begin the row k2.

FACINGS

Unlike ribbon or fabric, a knitted stockinette facing will be flexible and a perfect color match. For the front edges of a jacket or cardigan, the facing is best worked in one with the main part. To make sure that the facing folds on the same stitch along its length, slip this stitch on every right-side row.

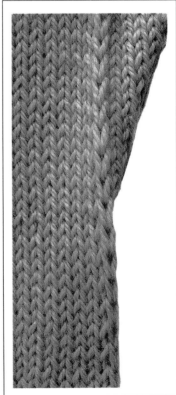

The slipped stitch forms a natural fold line for a facing.

Grafting

Duplicating a row of stitches with yarn and a wool needle makes an invisible join in knitting. Use this technique to alter the length of a garment or adapt the method to join shoulder seams.

Always use a blunt-pointed needle to avoid splitting stitches and thread it with enough yarn to work a row. Tension the sewn stitches to match the knitting. To make an alteration, snip a stitch in the center of the row, then pick up the loops of the stitches above and the stitches of the row below as you ease out the yarn.

Working on the stitches of the lower piece, undo rows to make it shorter or add more rows to make it longer. When you're ready to graft, lay the pieces to be joined close together, with the needles pointing in the same direction. It's easiest to graft in stockinette or reverse stockinette stitch, as described here, but once you understand how to imitate the stitches you can try grafting in other stitch patterns.

KNIT GRAFTING

Lay the pieces to be joined flat, with the right sides facing, so you can slip the stitches off the knitting needles as you trap them with the sewn stitches.

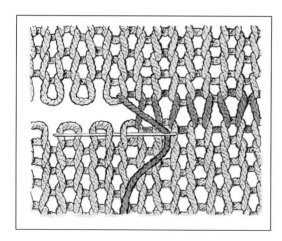

Bring the needle up through the first stitch of the last row on the lower piece. Go down through the loop at the side edge and up in the center of the next loop on the upper piece, then go down through the first stitch of the lower piece again, and up through the next stitch. Continue until all stitches and loops are joined to make a row.

PURL GRAFTING

Arrange the knitting on two needles and lay it flat. The sewn stitches will make a purl row.

Bring the needle down through the first stitch on the lower piece, up through the loop at the side edge, and down in the center of the next loop on the upper piece. Then go up through the first stitch of the lower piece. Continue in this way along the row, tensioning the sewn stitches as you go.

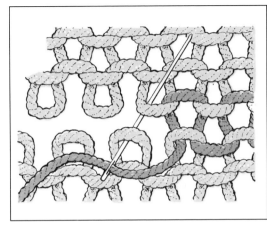

GRAFTING A SEAM

This variation on grafting is useful for joining shoulders. Because the stitches run in opposite directions, the side edges will be a half-stitch out, but this can be hidden in a seam.

Thread a wool needle with yarn and bring it up through the center of the first stitch on the front. Take it under the edge stitch on the back and down through the first stitch again. Repeat, taking in a whole stitch each time to match the front and back stitches perfectly.

```
TIP
FOR A PROFESSIONAL
RESULT

• When you're undoing from the
center of a row, use two circular
needles: one to pick up the
stitches below and the other for
the loops above.
```

Turning Rows

Short rows, made by turning and leaving stitches unworked, can be used to shape knitting.

For a steep slant, leave one or two stitches; for a gentler slope, leave more stitches unworked. For a symmetrical shaping, leave stitches unworked at both ends. For a smooth transition between rows, anchor the yarn before turning and working back.

1 Knit the number of stitches needed for the short row, bring the yarn forward, slip the next stitch purlwise, then take the yarn back.

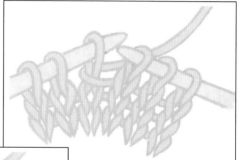

2 Return the slipped stitch to the left needle, ready to turn and work the next short row.

This swatch shows the use of turning rows to make a sloping edge. The stripes help you to see clearly where the yarn is taken around the slipped stitches. The same technique can be used when turning on a purl row.

More Useful Decreases

Working three stitches together keeps rib and other stitch patterns correct when decreasing and can be used decoratively and structurally for lace and solid-stitch patterns.

Choosing the right decrease for the stitch pattern is vital for shaping garments successfully. The single decreases shown on page 39 reduce the width of the knitting one stitch at a time, but sometimes it's necessary to take more stitches together.

A double decrease takes in the knitting more rapidly. In knit one, purl one rib, it can be placed so that the pattern is not interrupted on the next row. And in many stitch patterns, double decreases are used with double increases to create beautiful lacy effects.

All these methods of decreasing can be adapted to make multiple decreases by taking more stitches together. As with all decreases, it's very important to be aware of the position of the stitch that lies on top. Always pair a left-slanting and a right-slanting decrease when shaping a garment or working a stitch pattern. The dominant center stitch of the balanced double decrease makes a design feature of shaped darts and gives a clean line to lace patterns.

TIP
FOR A PROFESSIONAL RESULT

• Purling several stitches together is easier than knitting them together, so try to finish off large bobbles with a purl stitch.

RIGHT-SLANTING DECREASES

The easiest way to decrease two stitches is simply to knit three stitches together. With this decrease, the stitch furthest to the left will lie on top, giving a decrease that slants to the right. To give the same right-slanting decrease when working on the wrong side, you'll need to pull the stitches together.

Knit three together

Count the number of stitches to work into on the left needle. Insert the right needle tip into the front of the third stitch, then through the fronts of the other two stitches, take the yarn around the needle in the usual way, draw the new stitch through all three stitches, and drop them off the left needle together.

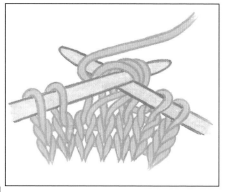

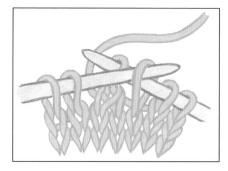

Purl three together

Insert the right needle into the fronts of stitches, take the yarn around the needle, and draw the new stitch through in the usual way, dropping the stitches off the left needle together.

LEFT-SLANTING DECREASES

For a double decrease that slants to the left, worked on a right-side row, you'll need to take the first stitch over a single decrease. For a similar-looking decrease worked on a wrong-side row, purl three together through the back of the loops.

Slip one, knit two together, pass the slipped stitch over

Slip the first stitch knitwise, knit the next two stitches together, then lift the first stitch over as shown here.

The first stitch lies on top, so the decrease slants to the left.

BALANCED DOUBLE DECREASE

Working a decrease that takes one stitch from each side and leaves the center stitch on top has lots of potential for shaping and for working beautiful stitch patterns.

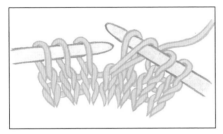

1 Insert the right needle into the second and first stitches as if to knit two together and slip these stitches onto the right needle.

2 Knit the next stitch, then lift the two slipped stitches over — the middle stitch of the decrease lies on top.

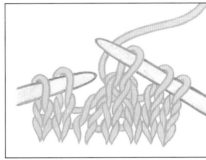

To balance decreases at each side of the fabric, as shown above, work the fifth rib, knit three together at the beginning of the row, and at the end of the row slip one, knit two together, and pass the slipped stitch over the fifth rib. Because the decreases reduce three stitches to one each time, the rib pattern is correct on the following rows.

In this swatch, the ribs travel to the center and the decreased stitches are neatly hidden under the center stitch. The rib remains correct for the following rows.

More Useful Increases

The basic increases shown on page 35 all make one stitch. Here are two neat ways to increase two stitches.

Multiple increases are useful for lace stitches and for keeping stitch patterns—such as ribs—correct while shaping.

Shaping in single rib looks very decorative when double lifted increases are used. To keep the rib correct, knit into the lifted stitches to make knit stitches, and purl into the lifted stitches to make purl stitches.

WORKING TWICE INTO A YARN-OVER

If your instructions tell you to make two stitches from a double yarn-over on the previous row, try this neat way of pairing the made stitches.

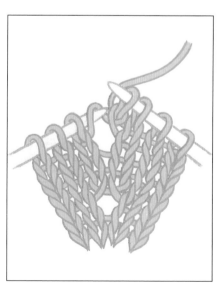

Work to the yarn-over, then knit into the back of the loop. Drop the second yarn-over off the left needle, then pick it up with the left needle, as shown, so that it is turned the other way, and knit into the front of it. The two stitches make a neat inverted V-shape over the hole.

WORKING A DOUBLE LIFTED STITCH INCREASE

Knitting into each side of the top of the stitch on the row below makes an increase that's decorative and useful for keeping patterns such as rib and moss stitch correct when shaping. This increase can be varied by knitting into the back of the lifted stitch or purling into the lifted stitch.

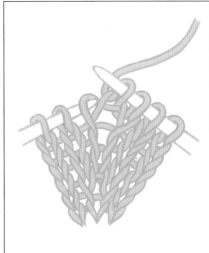

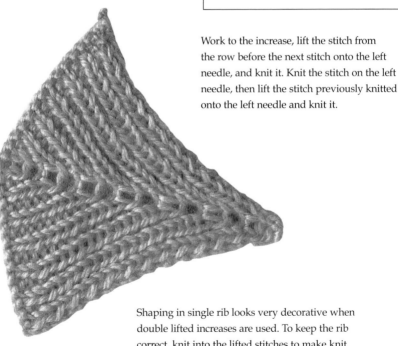

Work to the increase, lift the stitch from the row before the next stitch onto the left needle, and knit it. Knit the stitch on the left needle, then lift the stitch previously knitted onto the left needle and knit it.

Shaping in single rib looks very decorative when double lifted increases are used. To keep the rib correct, knit into the lifted stitches to make knit stitches and purl into the lifted stitches to make purl stitches.

Bias and Chevron Knitting

Use increases and decreases to shape within the fabric of your knitting to create bias and chevron effects.

If you increase and decrease one stitch at opposite ends on alternate rows so that the stitch count remains constant, the knitted fabric will slant while the direction of the stitches remains vertical.

Decreases at the beginning and increases at the end of a row tilt the fabric to the left, increases at the beginning and decreases at the end tilt the fabric to the right. Although often used to make flexible facings, this principle can be used to shape knitted fabrics of any size. The examples shown here are in stockinette stitch—the stripes are used to emphasize the slant—but textured stitch patterns and color motifs can also be shaped in this way. The angle of the slant can be varied by spacing the shapings further apart.

Put left and right bias shapings together to make a chevron fabric, with the stitches fanning out from or traveling into the center. You'll need to work a double increase or decrease at the center—or use single shapings on each side of one or more center stitches. A single chevron can be used to create a knitted fabric of any size or you can combine upward- and downward-pointing chevrons to make stitch patterns.

TIP
FOR A PROFESSIONAL RESULT

• Try bias knitting in a stranded color pattern—the motifs will seem to move to the left or right, depending on the shapings.

BIAS KNITTING

To make a flexible bias strip, cast on a few stitches and work the increases and decreases one or two stitches in from each end.

For a slant to the left, decrease one stitch at the beginning and increase one stitch at the end of each right-side row.

For a slant to the right, increase one stitch at the beginning and decrease one stitch at the end of each right-side row.

CHEVRON KNITTING

These examples are in stockinette, with shaping on every right-side row, but you can vary the spacing of the increases and decreases to suit your stitch pattern.

Below: Increasing at each side of the center stitch and decreasing at each end of every right-side row makes the stitches fan out from the center and forms an upward-pointing chevron.

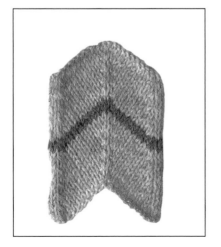

Above: Double decreasing at the center and increasing at each end of every right-side row makes the stitches travel to the center and forms a downward-pointing chevron.

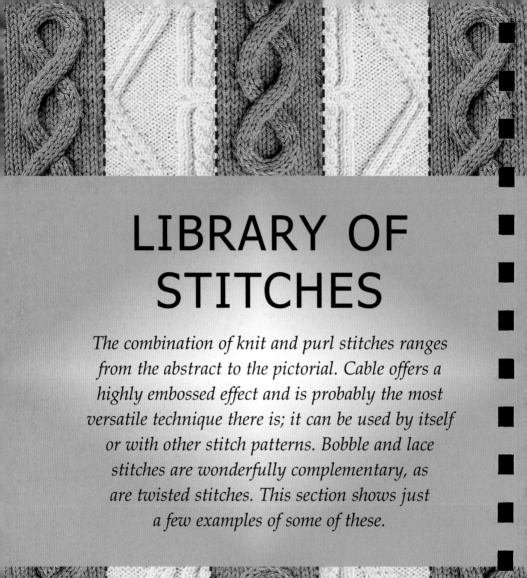

LIBRARY OF STITCHES

The combination of knit and purl stitches ranges from the abstract to the pictorial. Cable offers a highly embossed effect and is probably the most versatile technique there is; it can be used by itself or with other stitch patterns. Bobble and lace stitches are wonderfully complementary, as are twisted stitches. This section shows just a few examples of some of these.

KNIT AND PURL STITCHES

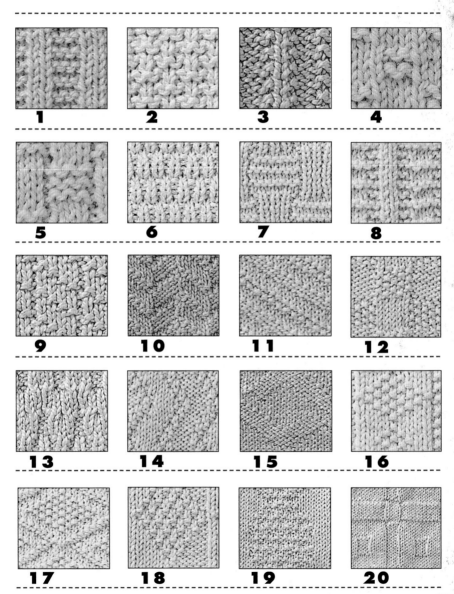

CABLE STITCHES

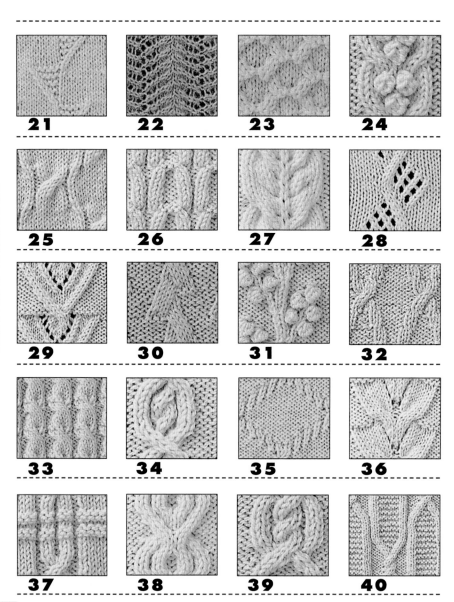

21

22

23

24

25

26

27

28

29

30

31

32

33

34

35

36

37

38

39

40

CABLE STITCHES

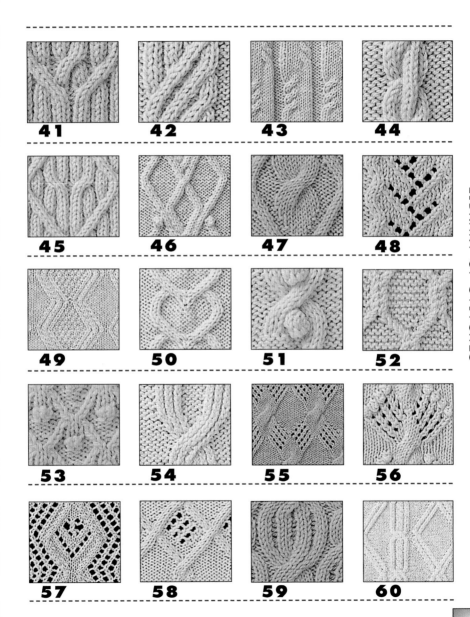

41 42 43 44

45 46 47 48

49 50 51 52

53 54 55 56

57 58 59 60

LACE AND BOBBLE STITCHES

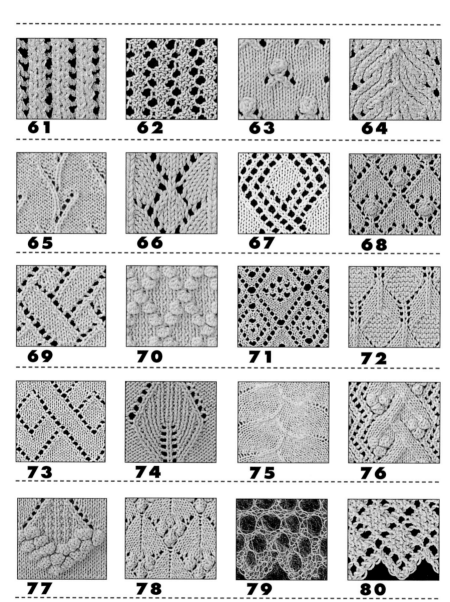

61

62

63

64

65

66

67

68

69

70

71

72

73

74

75

76

77

78

79

80

TWISTED AND OTHER STITCHES

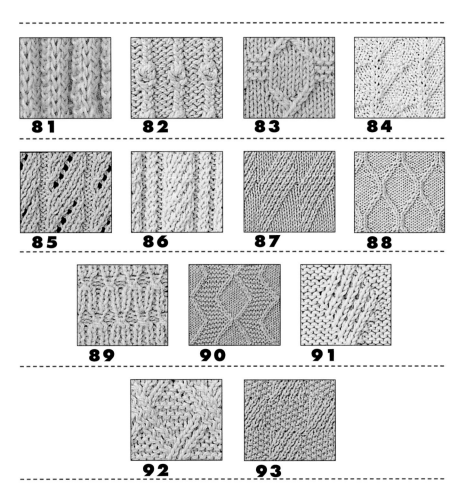

81

82

83

84

85

86

87

88

89

90

91

92

93

How to Use the Charts

Working from charts has many advantages, the main one being the immediacy with which the relationship between stitches and rows is illustrated.

By illustrating the relationship between the stitches and rows in a consistent manner, charts make understanding the construction of a stitch pattern and memorizing a repeat much easier. It's also an incentive to adapt existing stitches and invent new ones.

Because the number of different symbols used in any one stitch pattern is small, they can be learned a few at a time as required. All the symbols used here have been chosen to be pictorial rather than abstract representations of a stitch or technique.

CHART A
• Each square of the chart represents a stitch and each row of squares represents a row of stitches.
• The numbers up the sides of the chart are row numbers and therefore progress from the bottom to the top like the knitted sample.
• Rows that are numbered on the right-hand side of the chart are read from that side and represent right-side rows.
• Rows that are numbered on the left-hand side of the chart are read from that side and represent wrong-side rows. It helps to get into the habit of reading all charts this way, and it's essential when working patterns that are not symmetrical. Thus, Chart A reads:

1st row (right side): k5, p1, k1. (Worked from right to left.)
2nd row: p1, k1, p5. (Worked from left to right.)

Chart A

3rd row: k4, p1, k2. (Worked from right to left.)
4th row: p2, k1, p4 . . . and so on, reading right-side rows from the right and wrong-side rows from the left.

• If a stitch pattern is to be worked in the round, with right side facing, all rows are read from the right-hand side.

CHART B

Each symbol within a square indicates the way a stitch is worked. Initially, it may seem confusing that a blank square represents two stitches — knit on a right-side row and purl on a wrong-side row — and that a dot represents two stitches — purl on a right-side row and knit on a wrong-side row. But comparing a knitted sample with its chart immediately reveals the logic of this method. The blank squares convey the appearance of the smooth side of the stitch, as in stockinette stitch, and the dotted squares convey the appearance of the rounded side of the stitch, as in reverse stockinette stitch — see charts and samples Bi (right) and Bii (on next page). All that's needed to know whether a stitch is knit or purl is to know which side of the fabric is being worked.

CHART C

Cable symbols extend over the number of stitches involved in the cable cross, so the cable glossary runs from the smallest cables, which require only two stitches, to those requiring nine stitches. As far as possible, the symbols are drawn to look like the resulting cable. In this collection, cables are worked on right-side rows only, so it helps to remember that diagonals that slope backward (i.e., toward the beginning of the row) have the cable needle held at the back of the work and diagonals that slope forward (i.e., toward the end of the

Chart Bi

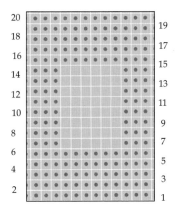

Chart Bii

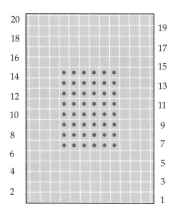

row) have the cable needle held at the front of the work. Thus, in chart Ci the symbol represents sl (slip) 2 sts onto cable needle and hold at back, k2, then k2 from cable needle. In chart Cii, the symbol represents sl 2 sts onto cable needle and hold at front, k2, then k2 from cable needle.

CHARTS D AND E

To make some charts look more like the resulting cable stitches, additional lines have been drawn in. These are merely to help the eye distinguish between one group of stitches and another and do not affect the working of the stitches. In the same way, lines have been used to distinguish one area from another where symbols are very dense and might be difficult to follow.

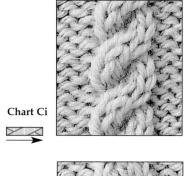

Chart Ci

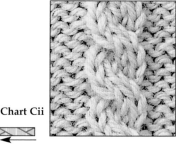

Chart Cii

CHART F

A blocked-out square represents no stitch at all. For example, a stitch lost by decreasing and not

Chart D   **Chart E**

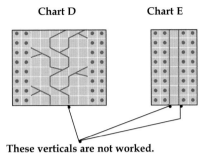

These verticals are not worked.

Any exceptional symbols are explained beside the relevant chart.

Chart F

compensated for with an increase. These blocked-out areas are not to be included in any stitch count, and any loss of vertical alignment of stitches in the chart must be ignored.

Thus, F shows a chart that begins with 5 sts, increases 2 sts on both rows 3 and 5, is worked over 9 sts on rows 6, 7, and 8 before decreasing 2 sts on both rows 9 and 11 to return to 5 sts on row 12.

CHART G

• An area of a chart that is unshaded and also has a bracket underneath indicates a group of stitches forming a repeat.
• A shaded area indicates stitches

Chart G

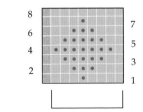

Multiple of 8 sts plus 1.

that are worked at the beginning or end of a row to balance the repeat.

• The number of stitches required for the repeat is given as a "Multiple of x sts" and the number of end stitches as "plus x" In chart G, "Multiple of 8 sts plus 1" means cast on a number of stitches divisible by 8 and add 1 more.

CHARTS H AND I

An unshaded area underlined by an H-shaped bracket indicates a panel or motif, and shaded areas indicate a notional number of stitches to the sides of the pattern area. In a panel, all the rows of the chart are repeated. A motif may have an odd number of rows, and any number of "background" rows may be worked below and above.

Chart H

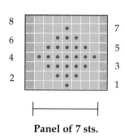

Panel of 7 sts.

Chart I

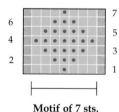

Motif of 7 sts.

Glossary of Symbols

ABBREVIATIONS

Alt	Alternate (i.e., every other row)
K	Knit
Psso	Pass slipped st(s) over
P	Purl
RS	Right side
Sl	Slip
St(s)	Stitch(es)
Tbl	Through back of loop(s)
Tog	Together
T2l	Twist 2 sts to left: take needle behind work, k in back loop of 2nd st on left-hand needle, k in front of first st; sl both sts off tog
T2r	Twist 2 sts to right: k2 tog leaving sts on needle, insert right-hand needle between sts just worked and k first st again; sl both sts from needle
WS	Wrong side
Yo	Yarn forward and over needle to make a st

K1 on right-side rows, p1 on wrong-side rows.

P1 on right-side rows, k1 on wrong-side rows.

K1 tbl on right-side rows, pl tbl on wrong-side rows.

K1 tbl on wrong-side rows.

Sl 1 st purlwise, with yarn behind work.

Sl 1 st purlwise, with yarn in front of work.

Yarn forward and over needle to make a st.

Make a st by picking up strand in front of next st and k it in back.

Make a st by picking up strand in front of next st and p it in back.

Increase 1 st by working k in front, then back of st.

Increase 1 st by working p in back, then front of st.

Increase 2 sts by working (k1, p1, k1) in st.

Increase 2 sts by working (k1 tbl, k1) in st, then insert left-hand needle behind the vertical strand running downward between the 2 sts just worked and work this strand k1 tbl.

Multiple increase—method given beside chart.

K2 tog on right-side rows, p2 tog on wrong-side rows.

Skpo on right-side rows, p2 tog tbl on wrong-side rows.

P2 tog on right-side rows, k2 tog on wrong-side rows.

P2 tog tbl on right-side rows.

K3 tog.

K3 tog tbl.

P3 tog.

Sl 1 knitwise, k2 tog, psso.

Sl 2 sts as if to work k2 tog; k1, psso.

Bind off 1 st.

St left on right-hand needle after binding off.

Knot: (k1, p1, k1, p1, k1) in st to make 5 sts from 1, then pass 2nd, 3rd, 4th, and 5th sts, one at a time, over first st.

Large knot: (k1, p1, k1, p1, k1, p1, k1) in st to make 7 sts from 1, pass 2nd, 3rd, 4th, 5th, 6th, and 7th sts, one at a time, over first st.

Small bobble: (k1, p1, k1, p1, k1) in st to make 5 sts from 1, turn, p5, turn; pass 2nd, 3rd, 4th, and 5th sts, one at a time, over first st, then k in back of this st.

Large bobble: (k1, p1, k1, p1, k1) in st to make 5 sts from 1, turn, p5, turn, k5, turn, p5, turn; pass 2nd, 3rd, 4th, and 5th sts over first st, then k in back of this st.

Purl bobble: (p in front, back, front, back, front) of st to make 5 sts from 1, turn, k5, turn, p5, turn, k5, turn; pass 2nd, 3rd, 4th, and 5th sts, one at a time, over first st, then k in back of this st.

Wide bobble: (k2, turn, p2, turn) twice (k next st tog with corresponding st of first row of bobble) twice.

Sl 3 sts onto cable needle, wind yarn counterclockwise around base of sts 8 times, ending with yarn at back of work, sl sts onto right-hand needle.

Sl 4 sts onto cable needle, wind yarn counterclockwise around base of sts 4 times, ending with yarn at back of work, sl sts onto right-hand needle.

Sl 5 sts onto cable needle, wind yarn counterclockwise around base of sts 4 times, ending with yarn at back of work, sl sts onto right-hand needle.

Sl 6 sts onto cable needle, wind yarn counterclockwise around base of sts 4 times, ending with yarn at back of work, sl sts onto right-hand needle.

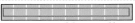

Sl 10 sts onto cable needle, wind yarn counterclockwise around base of sts 4 times, ending with yarn at back of work, sl sts onto right-hand needle.

No stitch.

Twist 2 sts to right: k2 tog, leaving sts on needle, insert right-hand needle between sts just worked and k first st again; sl both sts off tog.

Twist 2 sts to left: taking needle behind work, k in back loop of 2nd st on left-hand needle, k in front of first st; sl both sts off tog.

Purl twist to right: taking needle to front of work, k 2nd st on left-hand needle, p first st; sl both sts off tog.

Purl twist to left: taking needle behind work, p in back of 2nd st on left-hand needle, k in front of first st; sl both sts off tog.

Twist 3 sts; taking needle to front of work, k 3rd st on left-hand needle, then 2nd st, then first st; sl all sts off tog.

CABLES

Sl 1 st onto cable needle and hold back, k1, then k1 from cable needle.

Sl 1 st onto cable needle and hold at front, k1, then k1 from cable needle.

Sl 1 st onto cable needle and hold at back, k1, then p1 from cable needle.

Sl 1 st onto cable needle and hold at front, p1, then k1 from cable needle.

Sl 2 sts onto cable needle and hold at back, k1, then k2 from cable needle.

Sl 1 st onto cable needle and hold at front, k2, then k1 from cable needle.

Sl 2 sts onto cable needle and hold at back, k1, then p2 sts from cable needle.

Sl 1 st onto cable needle and hold at front, p2, then k1 st from cable needle.

Sl 2 sts onto cable needle and hold at back, k1, sl last st from cable needle back onto left-hand needle and p this st, then k1 from cable needle.

Sl 1 st onto cable needle and hold at front, k1, p1, then k1 from cable needle.

Sl 1 st onto cable needle and hold at back, k2, then k1 from cable needle.

Sl 2 sts onto cable needle and hold at front, k1, then k2 from cable needle.

Sl 1 st onto cable needle and hold at back, k2, then p1 from cable needle.

Sl 2 sts onto cable needle and hold at front, p1, then k2 from cable needle.

Sl 1 st onto cable needle and hold at back, t2r; then p1 from cable needle.

Sl 2 sts onto cable needle and hold at front, p1, then t2r from cable needle.

Sl 2 sts onto cable needle and hold at back, k2, then k2 from cable needle.

Sl 2 sts onto cable needle and hold at front, k2, then k2 from cable needle.

Sl 2 sts onto cable needle and hold at back, k2, then p2 from cable needle.

Sl 2 sts onto cable needle and hold at front, p2, then k2 from cable needle.

Sl 1 st onto cable needle and hold at back, k3, then p1 from cable needle.

Sl 3 sts onto cable needle and hold at front, p1, then k3 from cable needle.

Sl 3 sts onto cable needle and hold at back, k2, sl last st from cable needle back onto left-hand needle and k this st, then k2 from cable needle.

Sl 2 sts onto first cable needle and hold at front, sl 1 st onto 2nd cable needle and hold at back, k2; k1 from 2nd cable needle, then k2 from first cable needle.

Sl 3 sts onto cable needle and hold at back, k2, sl last st from cable needle back onto left-hand needle and p this st, then k2 from cable needle.

Sl 2 sts onto first cable needle and hold at front, sl 1 st onto 2nd cable needle and hold at back, k2; p1 from 2nd cable needle, then k2 from first cable needle.

Sl 1 st onto first cable needle and hold at front, sl 3 sts onto 2nd cable needle and hold at back, k1; p3 from 2nd cable needle, then k1 from first cable needle.

Sl 2 sts onto cable needle and hold at back, k3, then p2 from cable needle.

Sl 3 sts onto cable needle and hold at front, p2, then k3 from cable needle.

Sl 1 st onto cable needle and hold at back, t2r; t2l, then k1 from cable needle.

Sl 4 sts onto cable needle and hold at front, k1, then t2r, t2l from cable needle.

Sl 1 st onto cable needle and hold at back, t2r, t2l, then p1 from cable needle.

Sl 4 sts onto cable needle and hold at front, p1, then t2r, t2l from cable needle.

Sl 1 st onto cable needle and hold at back, t2l, t2r, then p1 from cable needle.

Sl 4 sts onto cable needle and hold at front, p1, then t2l, t2r from cable needle.

Sl 3 sts onto cable needle and hold

at back, k3, then k3 from cable needle.

Sl 3 sts onto cable needle and hold at front, k3, then k3 from cable needle.

Sl 4 sts onto cable needle and hold at back, k2, sl last 2 sts from cable needle back onto left-hand needle and p these 2 sts, then k2 from cable needle.

Sl 2 sts onto first cable needle and hold at front, sl 2 sts onto 2nd cable needle and hold at back, k2; p2 from 2nd cable needle, then k2 from first cable needle.

Sl 4 sts onto cable needle and hold at back, k3, sl last st from cable needle back onto left-hand needle and k this st, then k3 from cable needle.

Sl 4 sts onto cable needle and hold at back, k3, sl last st from cable needle back onto left-hand needle and p this st, then k3 from cable needle.

Sl 4 sts onto cable needle and hold at back, k4, then k4 from cable needle.

Sl 5 sts onto cable needle and hold at back, k4, then k5 from cable needle.

Sl 4 sts onto cable needle and hold at back, k5, then k4 from cable needle.

KNIT AND PURL STITCHES

Knit and purl stitches are the basis of all knitting. On their own they offer a tremendous number of possibilities. The smoothness of the "knit" side of the stitch and the roundness of the "purl" side can be contrasted to make textures as varied as seed stitch and brocade. The stitches can be aligned vertically to make ribs or horizontally to make ridges. In turn, these can be combined to make brick patterns and basket weaves.

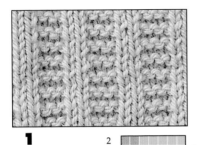

1

2 | | | 1

Multiple of 5 sts plus 2.

1st row (right side): * k2, p3;
repeat from * to last 2 sts, k2.
2nd row: p.
Repeat rows 1 and 2.

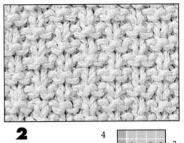

4

8
6
4
2

7
5
3
1

Multiple of 6 sts plus 4.

1st and 3rd rows (right side): *
k1, p2, k3; repeat from * to last 4
sts, k1, p2, k1.
2nd and alt rows: p.
5th and 7th rows: * k4, p2; repeat
from * to last 4 sts, k4.
8th row: p.
Repeat rows 1–8.

2

4
2

3
1

Multiple of 4 sts plus 1.

1st row (right side): * k1, p3;
repeat from * to last st, k1.
2nd row: p.
3rd row: * p2. k1, p1; repeat from
* to last st, p1.
4th row: p.
Repeat rows 1–4.

3

2 | | 1

Multiple of 8 sts plus 5.

1st row (right side): * p2, k1,
p2, k3; repeat from * to last 5 sts,
p2, k1, p2.
2nd row: k5, * k1, p1, k6;
repeat from * to end.
Repeat rows 1 and 2.

5

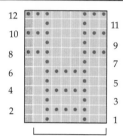

Multiple of 8 sts plus 1.

1st, 3rd, 5th, and 7th rows (right side): * k2, p1, k3, p1, k1; repeat from * to last st, k1.
2nd, 4th, and 6th rows: p1, * p1, k5, p2; repeat from * to end.
8th and 10th rows: k1, * k2, p3, k3; repeat from * to end.
9th and 11th rows: k2, p1, k3, p1, k1; repeat from * to last st, k1.
12th row: as 8th row.
Repeat rows 1–12.

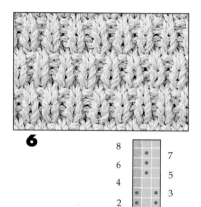

6

Multiple of 2 sts plus 1.

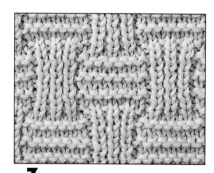

7

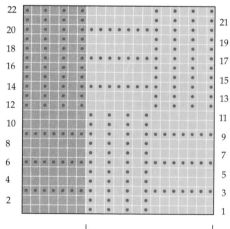

Multiple of 14 sts plus 7.

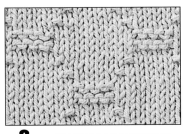

8

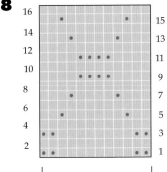

Multiple of 12 sts.

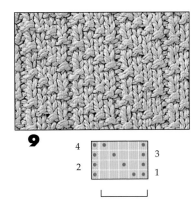

9

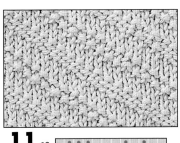

Multiple of 5 sts plus 1.

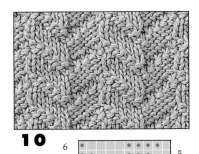

10

Multiple of 10 sts.

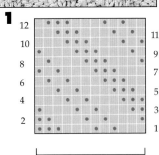

11

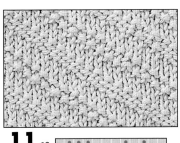

Multiple of 12 sts.

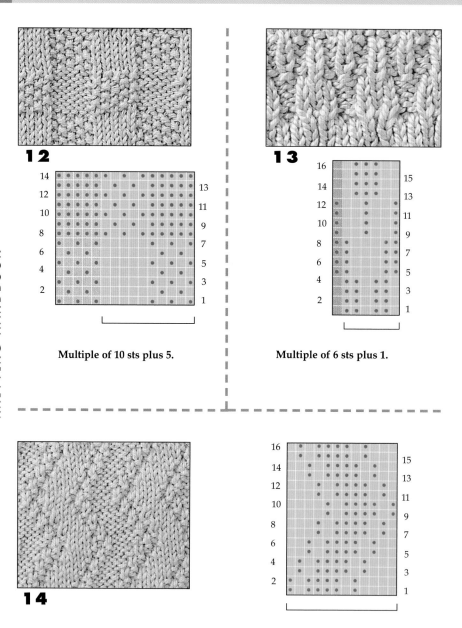

12

Multiple of 10 sts plus 5.

13

Multiple of 6 sts plus 1.

14

Multiple of 12 sts. This stitch is reversible.

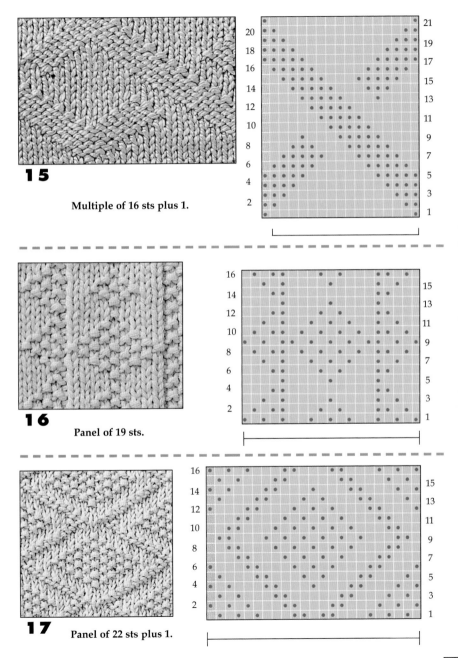

15

Multiple of 16 sts plus 1.

16

Panel of 19 sts.

17

Panel of 22 sts plus 1.

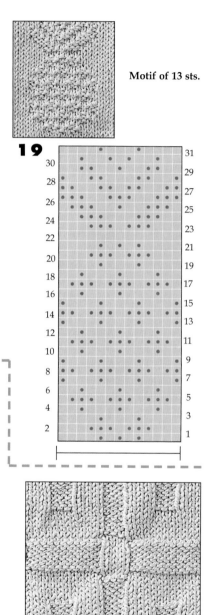

18

Multiple
of 12 sts.

This
stitch is
reversible.

20 19 18 17 16 15 14 13 12 11 10 9 8 7 6 5 4 3 2 1

Motif of 13 sts.

19

31 30 29 28 27 26 25 24 23 22 21 20 19 18 17 16 15 14 13 12 11 10 9 8 7 6 5 4 3 2 1

24 23 22 21 20 19 18 17 16 15 14 13 12 11 10 9 8 7 6 5 4 3 2 1

Multiple of 16 sts plus 4.

20

CABLE STITCHES

Cables are stitches that look like twisted ropes, interwoven plaits, and crisscross trellises and which seem so complicated to the uninitiated. The principle is simple: Making a cable is merely working stitches, or groups of stitches, out of sequence. Cables are usually worked in stockinette stitch on a plain or textured ground, but they look particularly rich when they themselves are textured.

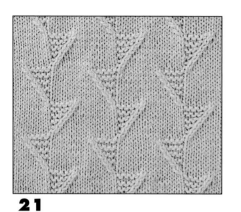

21

Multiple of 14 sts plus 2.

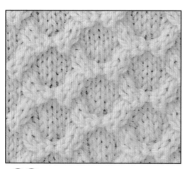

22

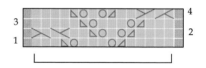

Multiple of 15 sts plus 2.

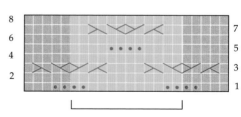

Multiple of 12 sts plus 10.

23

24

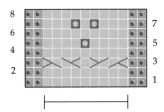

Panel of 9 sts.

**25**

Multiple of 23 sts plus 11.

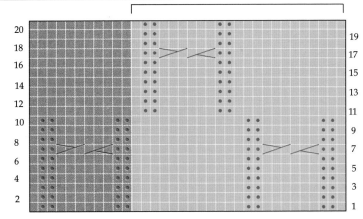

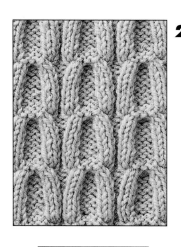

26

27

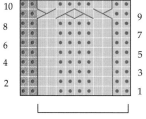

10
8
6
4
2

9
7
5
3
1

Multiple of 10 sts plus 2.

12
10
8
6
4
2

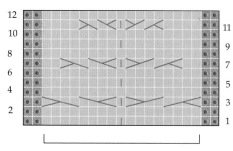

11
9
7
5
3
1

Panel of 17 sts.

REMINDER

• Sl next 2 sts onto cable needle and hold at front, k2, then p2 from cable needle.

• Sl next 2 sts onto cable needle and hold back, p2, then k2 from cable needle.

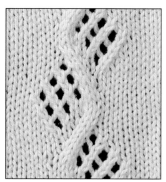

28

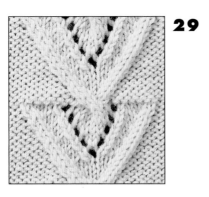

29

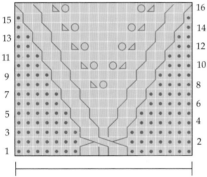

Panel of 19 sts.

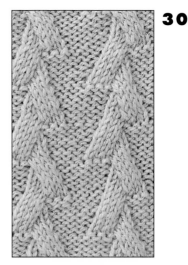

30

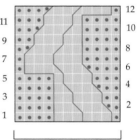

Multiple of 11 sts.

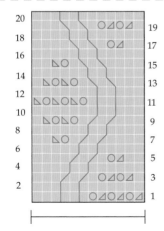

Panel of 12 sts.

TIP
FOR A PROFESSIONAL RESULT

• Counting rows between cables can be tricky. Slip a marker of contrast yarn between stitches on the cable row and pull it out afterward.

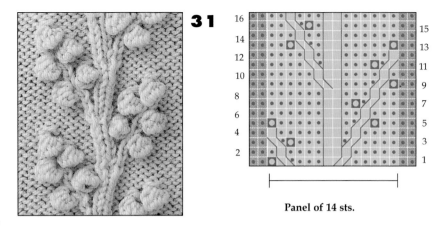

31

Panel of 14 sts.

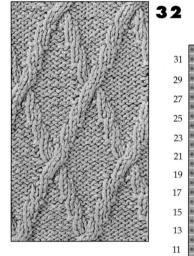

32

Multiple of 12 sts plus 13.

33

34

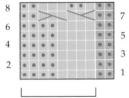

8								7
6								5
4								3
2								1

Multiple of 8 sts plus 2.

REMINDER

• Sl 3 sts onto cable needle and hold at front, k1, p2, then k3 from cable needle.

• Sl 2 sts onto cable needle and hold at front, sl next 4 sts onto 2nd cable needle and hold at back, k2, then k4 from 2nd cable needle, then k2 from first cable needle.

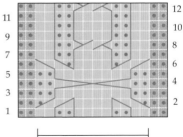

Panel of 12 sts.

113

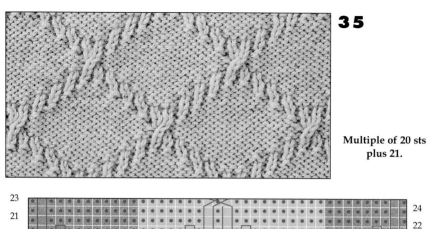

35

Multiple of 20 sts
plus 21.

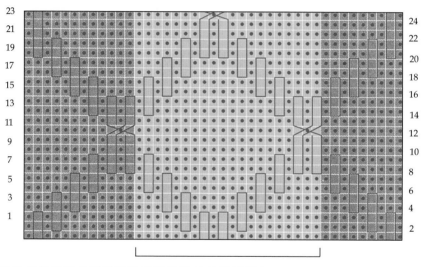

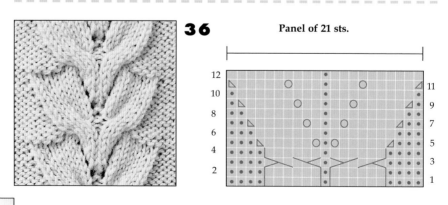

36

Panel of 21 sts.

37

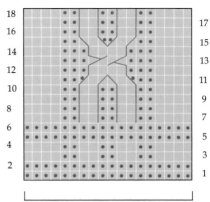

18
16
14
12
10
8
6
4
2

17
15
13
11
9
7
5
3
1

Multiple of 18 sts.

38

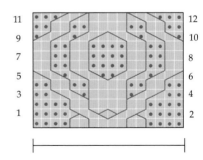

11
9
7
5
3
1

12
10
8
6
4
2

Panel of 16 sts.

39

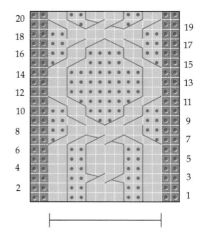

20					19
18					17
16					15
14					13
12					11
10					9
8					7
6					5
4					3
2					1

Panel of 12 sts.

40

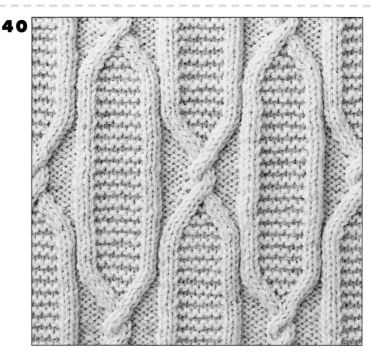

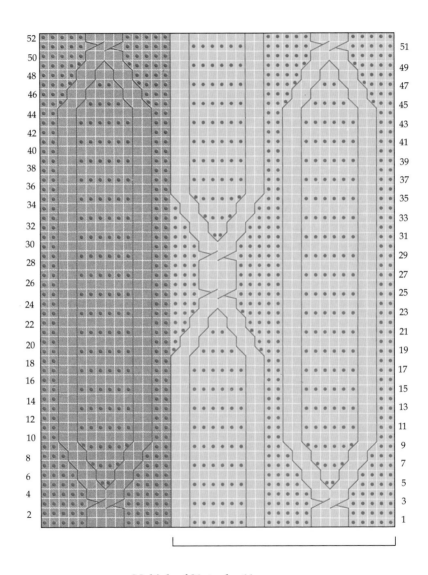

Multiple of 24 sts plus 14.

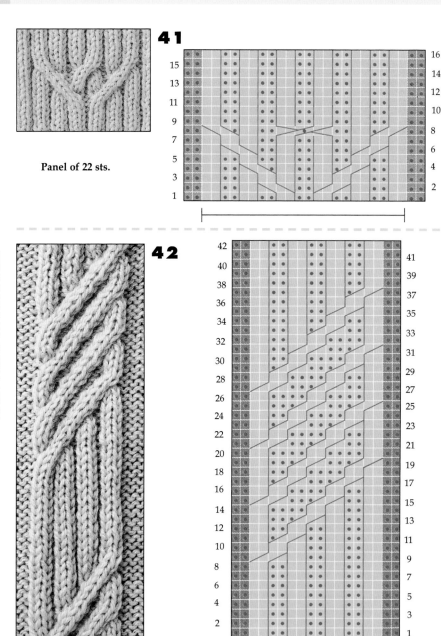

41

Panel of 22 sts.

42

Panel of 14 sts.

118

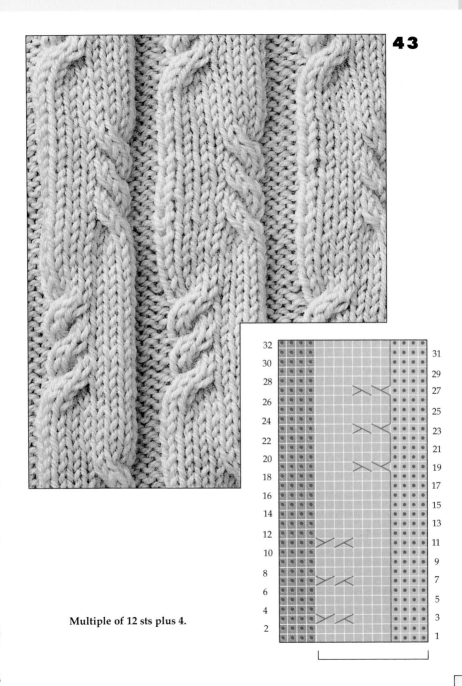

43

Multiple of 12 sts plus 4.

44

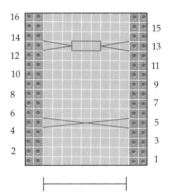

Panel of 9 sts.

REMINDER

• Sl 6 sts onto cable needle and hold at back, k3, sl last 3 sts from cable needle back onto left-hand needle, k3, then k3 sts from cable needle.

• Sl 3 sts onto first cable needle and hold at back, sl next 3 sts onto 2nd cable needle and hold at front, k3, k3 from 2nd cable needle, k3 from first cable needle.

45

Panel of 30 sts.

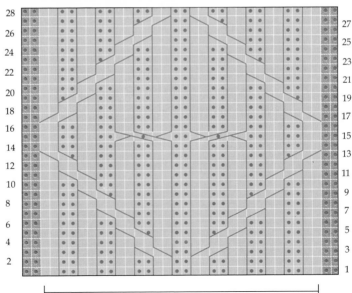

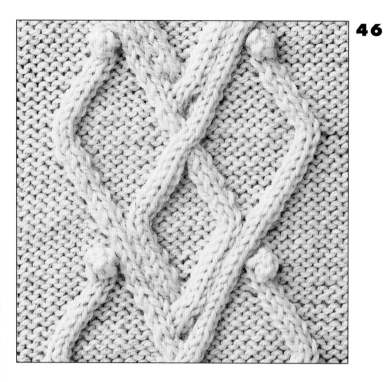

46

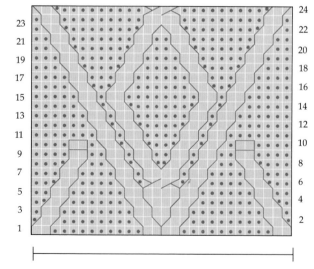

Panel of 28 sts.

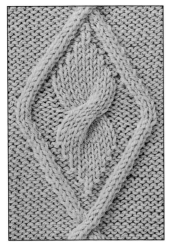

47

Panel of 23 sts.

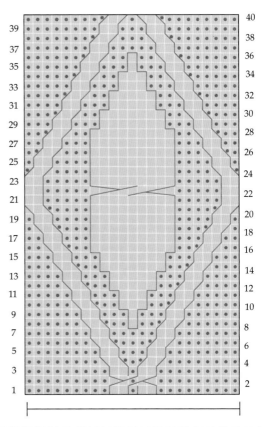

48

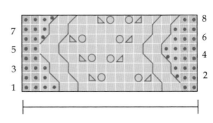

Panel of 15 sts.

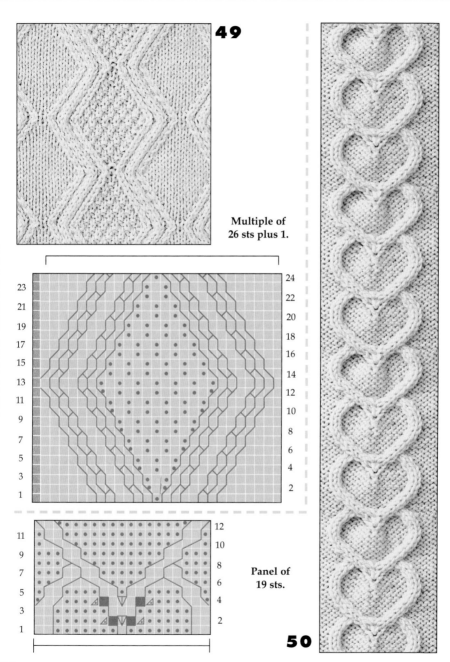

49

Multiple of
26 sts plus 1.

Panel of
19 sts.

50

51

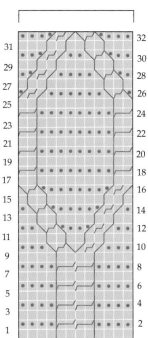

52

Multiple of 12 sts.

Panel of 19 sts.

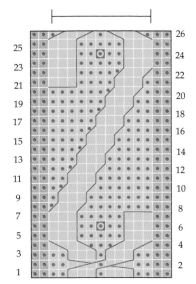

53

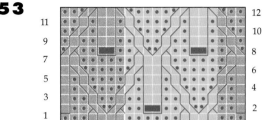

Multiple of 10 sts plus 10.

54

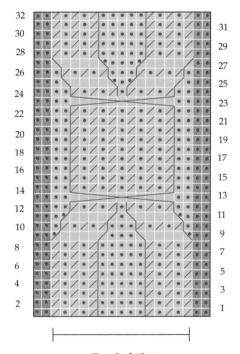

Panel of 15 sts.

REMINDER

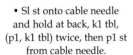

• Sl st onto cable needle and hold at back, k1 tbl, (p1, k1 tbl) twice, then p1 st from cable needle.

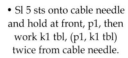

• Sl 5 sts onto cable needle and hold at front, p1, then work k1 tbl, (p1, k1 tbl) twice from cable needle.

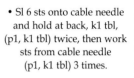

• Sl 6 sts onto cable needle and hold at back, k1 tbl, (p1, k1 tbl) twice, then work sts from cable needle (p1, k1 tbl) 3 times.

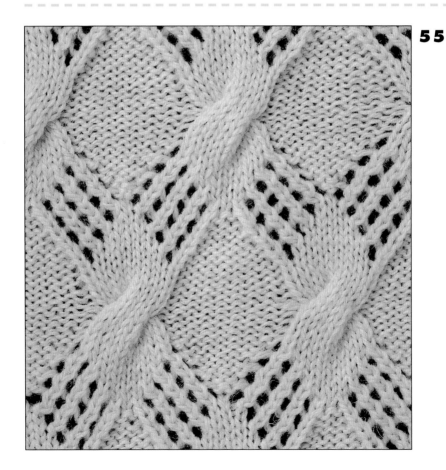

55

• CABLE STITCHES •

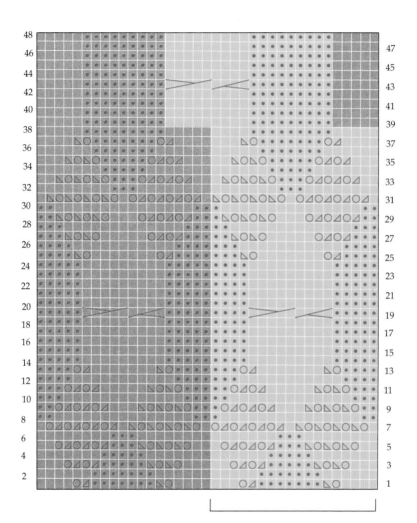

Multiple of 18 sts plus 19.

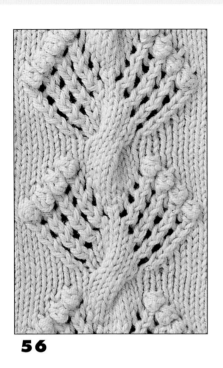

56

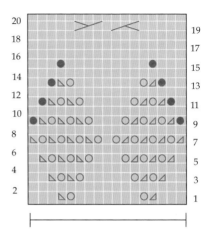

20

18

16

14

12

10

8

6

4

2

19

17

15

13

11

9

7

5

3

1

Panel of 17 sts.

REMINDER

• Sl next 3 sts onto cable needle and hold at back, k4, then k3 from cable needle.

57

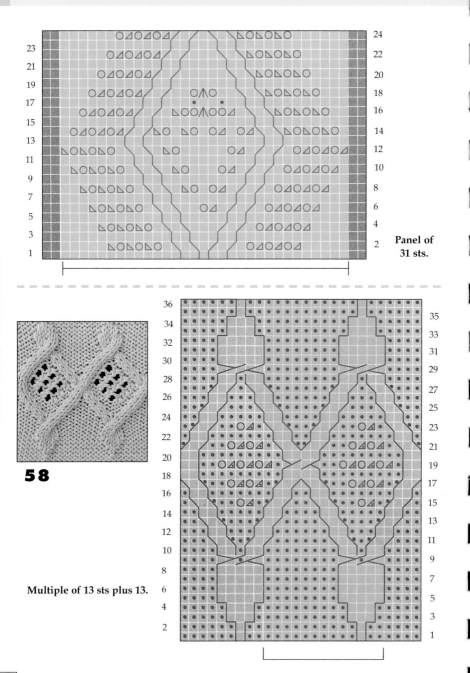

Panel of 31 sts.

58

Multiple of 13 sts plus 13.

59

REMINDER

- Sl 6 sts onto cable needle and hold at back, k2, p1, k2, then work sts from cable needle (p1, k2) twice.

✳

- Drop k st from needle to make ladder, then work yo. (Run will stop at previous yo.)

- Note that only rows 1–24 are repeated, foundation row is not. On last row make appropriate runs before binding off.

• CABLE STITCHES •

Multiple of 26 sts plus 15.

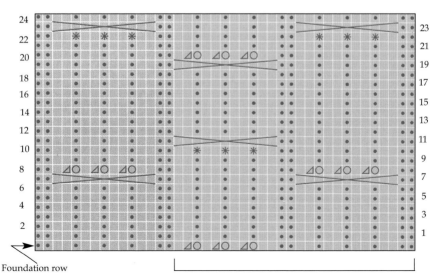

Foundation row

60

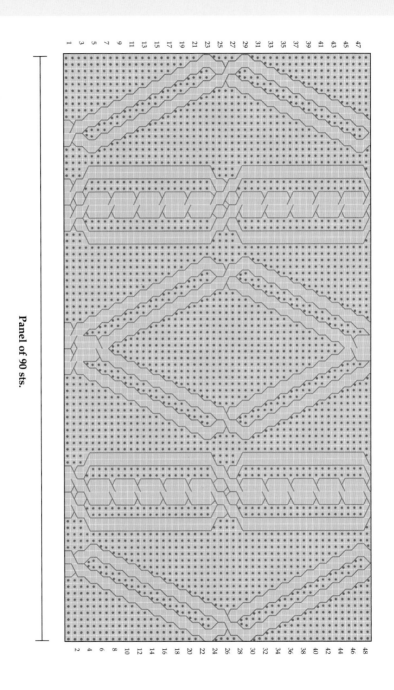

Panel of 90 sts.

LACE & BOBBLE STITCHES

*Both lace and bobble stitches are very
compatible with cables.
Bobble and eyelets can both be used to form an
allover lacy fabric or to define a pattern
on a solid ground.
Lace stitches are usually better worked on a largish
needle and in a yarn that can be shaped and pinned
out, then thoroughly pressed.*

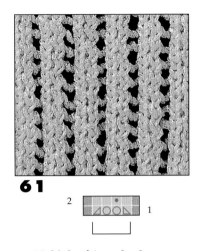

61

2 [diagram] 1

Multiple of 4 sts plus 2.

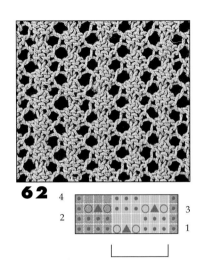

62

4 [diagram] 3
2 [diagram] 1

Multiple of 6 sts plus 5.

63

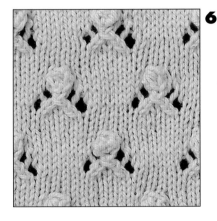

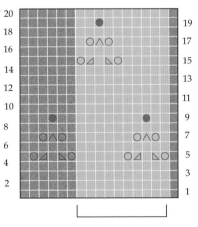

20		19
18	●	17
16	O∧O	15
14	O⊿ ⊾O	13
12		11
10	● ●	9
8	O∧O O∧O	7
6	O⊿ ⊾O O⊿ ⊾O	5
4		3
2		1

Multiple of 10 sts plus 7.

REMINDER

[symbol]

• Sl 3 sts onto cable needle and hold at front, k1, p2, then k3 from cable needle.

135

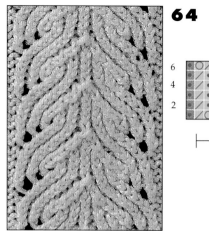

64

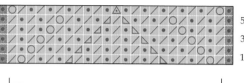

6
4
2

5
3
1

Panel of 23 sts.

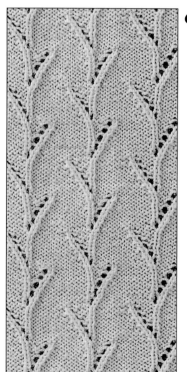

65

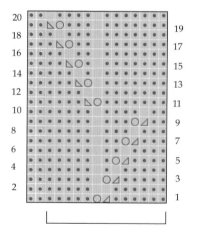

20
18
16
14
12
10
8
6
4
2

19
17
15
13
11
9
7
5
3
1

Multiple of 13 sts plus 2.

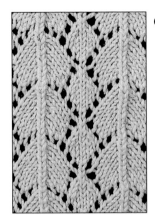

66

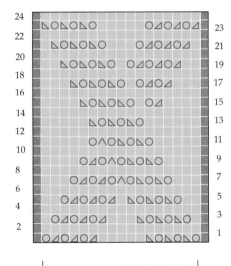

Multiple of 12 sts plus 13.

67

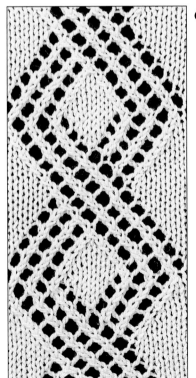

Panel of 17 sts.

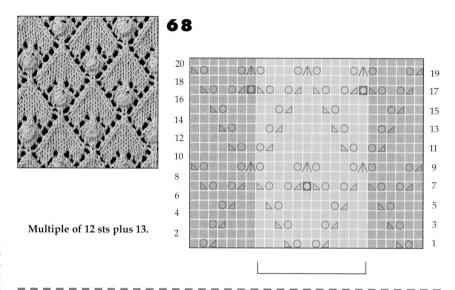

68

Multiple of 12 sts plus 13.

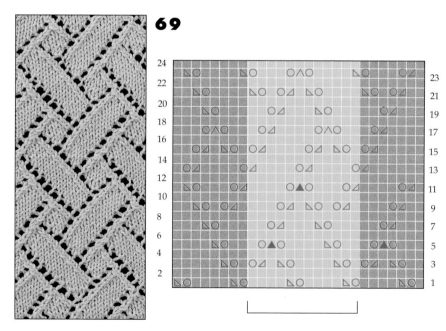

69

Multiple of 12 sts plus 15 sts.

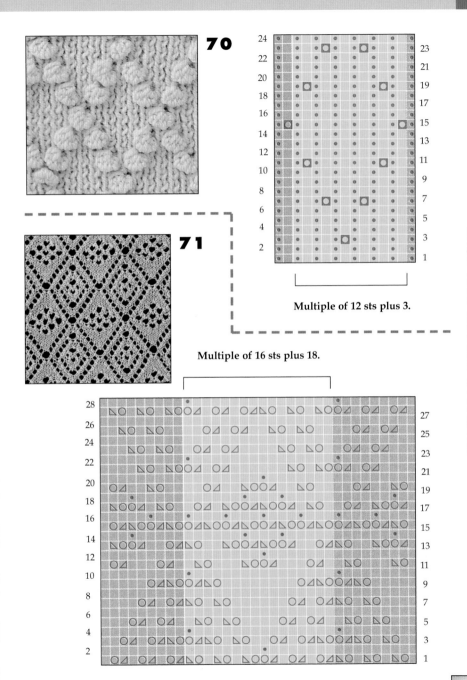

70

24 23
22 21
20 19
18 17
16 15
14 13
12 11
10 9
8 7
6 5
4 3
2 1

Multiple of 12 sts plus 3.

71

Multiple of 16 sts plus 18.

28 27
26 25
24 23
22 21
20 19
18 17
16 15
14 13
12 11
10 9
8 7
6 5
4 3
2 1

72

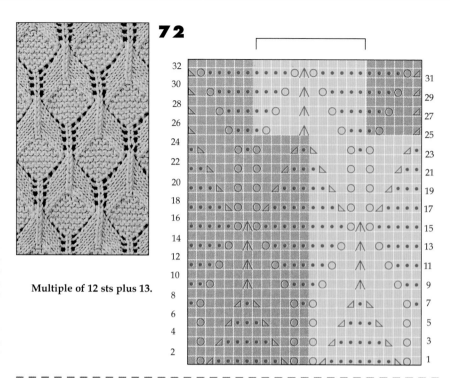

Multiple of 12 sts plus 13.

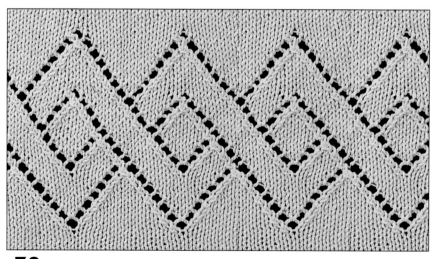

73

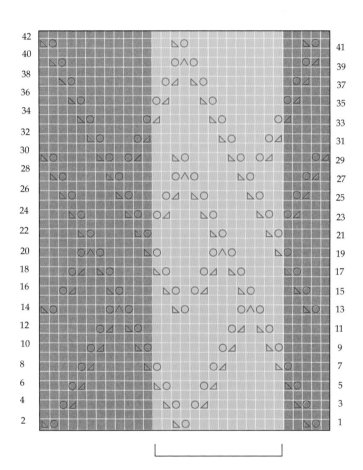

Multiple of 14 sts plus 17.

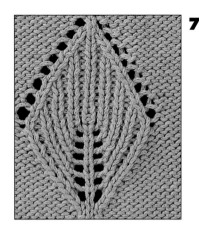

74

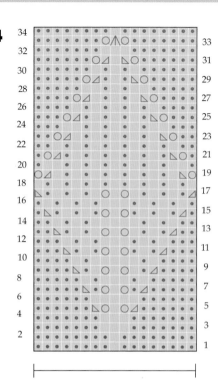

Motif of 17 sts.

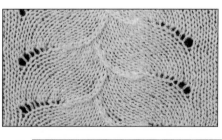

75

Panel of 37 sts.

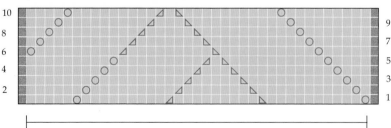

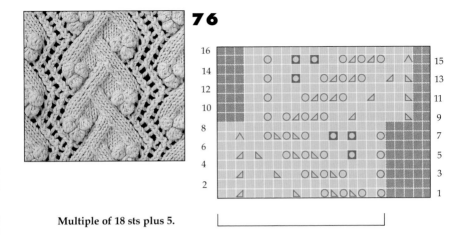

76

Multiple of 18 sts plus 5.

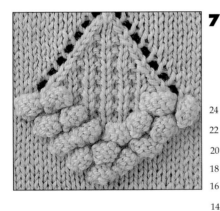

77

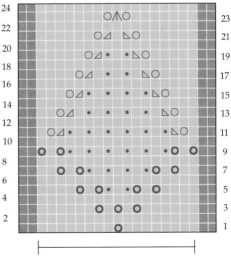

Motif of 17 sts.

78

Multiple of 13 sts plus 15.

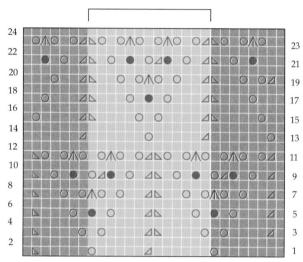

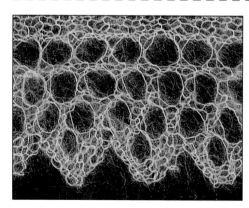

79

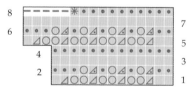

Cast on 11 sts.

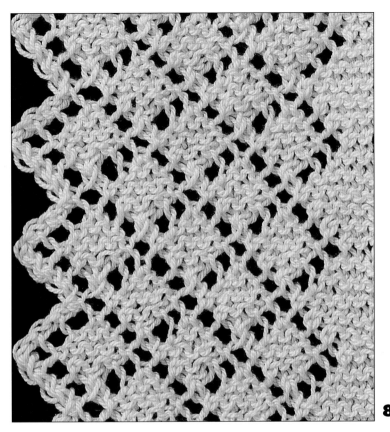

80

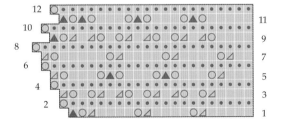

Cast on 22 sts.

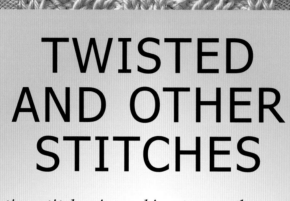

TWISTED AND OTHER STITCHES

Twisting stitches is working two or three stitches out of sequence, but without using a cable needle. This is an easy way to create patterns where lines of stitches travel over the surface of the knitting. They can be worked on right- or wrong-side rows, and the stitches can be all knit, all purl, or a combination of the two.

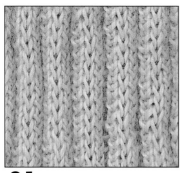

81

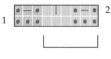

Multiple of 6 sts plus 3.
This stitch is reversible.

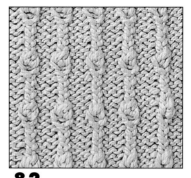

82

Multiple of
4 sts plus 3.

83

Multiple
of 9 sts
plus 3.

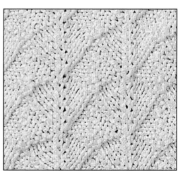

84

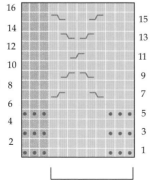

Multiple of 12 sts plus 1.

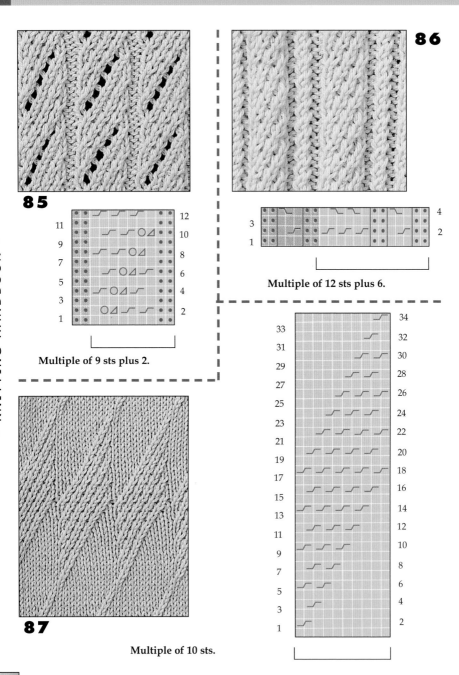

85

Multiple of 9 sts plus 2.

86

Multiple of 12 sts plus 6.

87

Multiple of 10 sts.

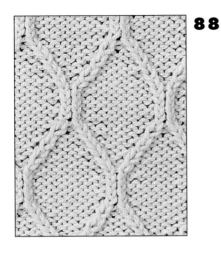

88

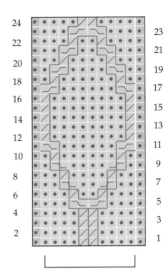

24   23
22   21
20   19
18   17
16   15
14   13
12   11
10   9
8   7
6   5
4   3
2   1

Multiple of 10 sts plus 10.

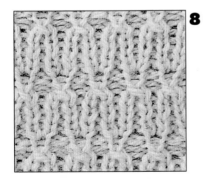

89

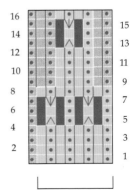

16   15
14   13
12   11
10   9
8   7
6   5
4   3
2   1

Multiple of 8 sts plus 1.
(Note that rows 9–16 are a
multiple of 4 sts plus 5.)

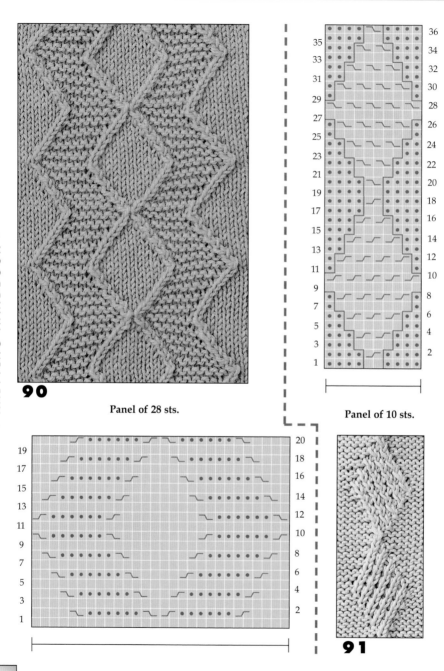

90

Panel of 28 sts.

Panel of 10 sts.

91

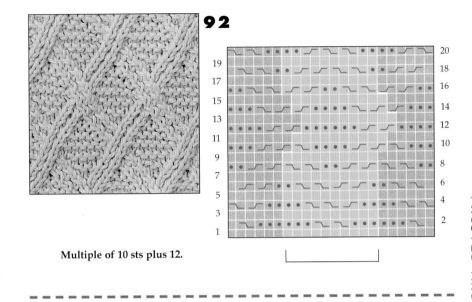

92

Multiple of 10 sts plus 12.

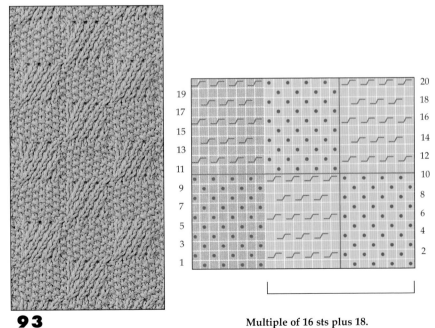

93

Multiple of 16 sts plus 18.

KNITTING WITH COLOR

All around the world, people have developed traditions of color knitting. Among the best known are patterns from the Shetland Islands, Scandinavia, Eastern Europe, and South America. Stranded color knitting is usually worked from a chart. Intarsia is simply working areas of color with separate balls of yarn that are linked together at each color change.

Stranded Color Knitting

Most stranded color knitting is worked in stockinette with just two colors in a row. One or both of these colors may be changed on subsequent rows. Some patterns use three—or even four—colors in a row, but this can make the fabric very thick.

Reading the chart as directed, count the squares in the first color and work that number of stitches. Then count and work the stitches in the second color. Continue counting and changing the colors along the row. Once you have established the first row, you can simply glance at the chart to see how the motifs change.

In many traditions, stranded color knitting is worked in the round, making it easy to see the pattern. If you're color knitting in the round, read each row of the chart from right to left. As you'll discover, most traditional patterns from the Shetland Islands change color after no more than seven stitches in a row, with the yarn not in use stranded loosely on the wrong side of the work. Stranding across more stitches would make an overly long strand, so it's best if the yarn not in use can be woven in at regular intervals to keep the wrong side tidy.

HOLDING THE YARNS

The simplest way to change colors is to drop one yarn and pick up the other. But for faster knitting, experiment with the following techniques.

HOLDING ONE YARN IN EACH HAND

Hold and work with one yarn in the right hand in the usual way. Tension the other yarn through the fingers of your left hand. To knit with the left-hand yarn, insert the right needle, dip it under the yarn, and pull it through with a hooking action. When purling, be careful not to twist stitches.

HOLDING BOTH YARNS IN ONE HAND

Hold both the yarns in the right hand, with the main color over the first finger and the contrast color tensioned over the middle fingertip. Knit in the usual way with the main color, then turn the hand slightly to flick the yarn from the middle finger around the needle for the contrast stitches. On purl rows you may find it easier to manipulate the main color between thumb and first finger and the contrast over the first finger, still with the same rocking action of the wrist to take each yarn around the needle.

STRANDING

The strands carried across should be tensioned loosely and evenly so that the knitting lies flat. Decide which color will lie on top and always strand the yarns in the same order.

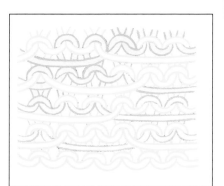

WEAVING

The yarn not in use can be woven over and under on alternate stitches on the wrong side, making a very firm fabric. Or it can be woven in after several stitches. Make sure the contrast color doesn't show through to the right side.

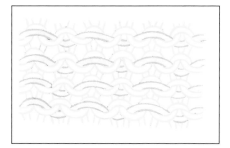

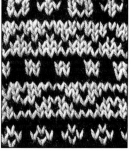

Left: These geometric patterns from the Shetlands, off the northern coast of Scotland, are called "peerie patterns."

Right: This star motif is instantly recognizable as a Shetland pattern by the shaded effect.

Multiple of 20 sts plus 1.

STARFLOWER WITH DIAMOND FLOWER BORDER

Here, instead of shading gently, the color changes in the motif and the background is made on the same row, which adds to the jazzy feel of this bright interpretation of a traditional star with peerie patterns.

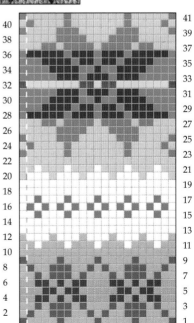

155

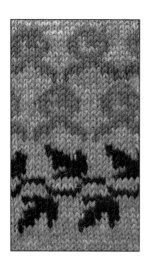

HAREBELLS AND VINE BORDER

The vine borders are shown running in opposite directions. If you want to knit the next band of harebells with the flowers facing right, read rows 9 to 31 in the opposite direction.

ROSEBUDS AND IVY BORDER

These very pretty patterns are inspired by Swedish mittens. Work rows 17 to 26 for just one row of rosebuds, or repeat rows 17 to 38 for an allover pattern.

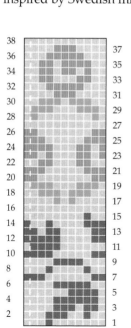

Multiple of 10 sts plus 1.

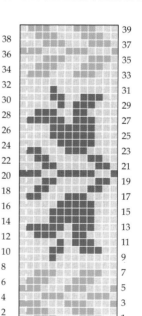

Multiple of 12 sts plus 1.

LARGE REINDEER

Although most of this pattern has been designed for stranded knitting, you'll find it easier to use separate balls of black for the reindeer body and one for each area in red between motifs.

Multiple of 30 sts plus 1.

Intarsia Color Knitting

Large geometric patterns, individual motifs, and picture knits are the kind of color designs that are best knitted using the intarsia technique.

Intarsia is simply working areas of color with separate balls of yarn that are linked together at each color change. This eliminates stranding or weaving in on the wrong side, and gives a single-thickness fabric. The technique is used for flat knitting only—intarsia cannot be worked in the round.

Designs in intarsia are worked from charts where the number of stitches in each color can be seen clearly and easily. Stockinette is the most frequently used stitch, but the technique works just as well with textured stitches and cables. Some designs—such as tiny blocks of color scattered on a plain background—are best worked in a combination of intarsia and stranding. Use separate lengths of yarn for small motifs, and strand the background color, twisting the yarns at each color change.

TIPS
FOR PROFESSIONAL RESULTS

• Reusable peel-off stickers are ideal for keeping your place in a chart. Position them above the row you're working from, so you can see how it relates to the pattern already knitted.

• Use bobbins to knit small areas of color.

ORGANIZING THE YARNS

First sort out the yarns by counting the number of areas in each color, then wind off suitable lengths of yarn according to the size of the areas. Use complete balls of yarn for each large area. Wind the yarn onto bobbins for smaller areas or, if there are just a few contrast stitches, use a short length of yarn. If the design is very complex, with lots of colors, avoid tangles by using lengths of yarn that can be pulled free easily because they are not attached to a ball or bobbin.

DIAGONAL COLOR CHANGES

It's easy to keep your knitting neat when working diagonals, because the colors move along one stitch each time. Linking the yarns at the changeover, therefore, comes naturally.

HOW TO LINK COLOR AREAS

Every time you change colors, you must link the areas together or there will be holes in your knitting. All you need to do is twist the yarns on the wrong side.

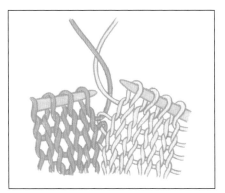

ON A KNIT ROW

Knit with the first color (here it's pink) to the changeover, then drop the yarn. Pick up the second color (purple) and take it around the first yarn before knitting the next stitch.

ON A PURL ROW

Purl with the second yarn to the changeover. Make sure you take the first yarn around the second yarn before knitting the next stitch.

VERTICAL COLOR CHANGES

When the colors change at the same place on several rows, be particularly careful to twist the yarns neatly and evenly to avoid holes and loose stitches. Darn in ends along color changes.

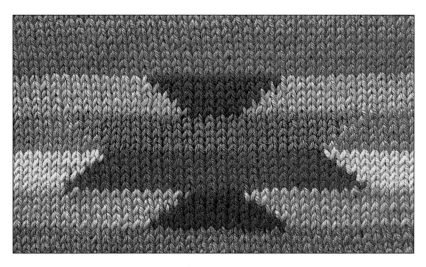

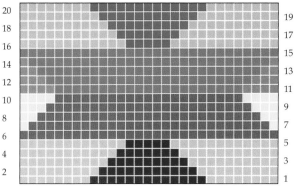

Motif of 29 sts.

BROKEN STRIPES

One of the simplest exercises in intarsia is to use a few diagonal color changes to make motifs within stripes. Try light on dark or dark on light tonal variations.

BUGS

These stylized insects are made more lively with a central stripe of a deeper color. Use one or all of them as a repeat pattern or as individual motifs.

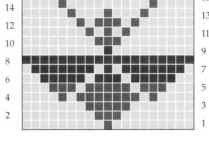

Motif of 15 sts.

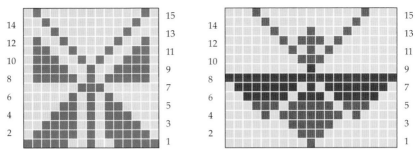

Motif of 19 sts.

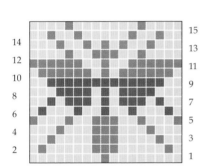

Motif of 17 sts.

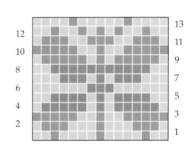

Motif of 15 sts.

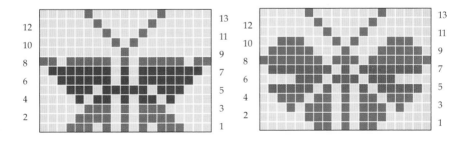

Motif of 19 sts.

Motif of 19 sts.

SOUTH AMERICAN BIRD

Based on a piece of Guatemalan weaving, this mixture of intarsia and stranded color knitting has a go-as-you-please border. The geometric repeat pattern avoids being too mechanical by having random color changes.

Motif of 39 sts.

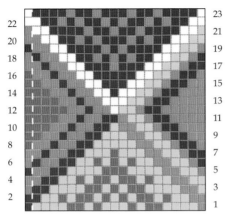

Motif of 20 sts plus 1.

LEAVES

Almost any pictorial image can be knitted. The chart looks taller than the motif because of the gauge.

Motif of 35 sts.

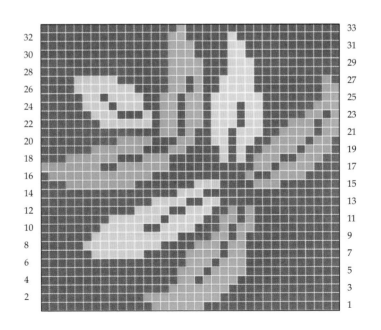

DESIGN YOUR OWN KNITS

Before you can create your own garments, you need to know how to translate measured shapes into knitting. This section will show you how to do this and how to work garments to the design you desire. Almost any flat or three-dimensional shape can be worked in knitting. All that is required is common sense, a calculator, and a tension square using the correct yarn, needles, and stitch pattern.

How to Design

Inventing a design is simply a matter of common sense, a few calculations, and your imagination! There are probably as many different ways of working out a set of instructions as there are designers, but here's some advice to get you started.

First, you need a source of inspiration. The idea for a design may be inspired by the texture of a yarn, an exciting range of colors, a fashion trend, a combination of stitch patterns, a motif, or a construction technique. Next, choose your yarn, experiment with stitch patterns, and knit up some swatches. When you're happy with the look and feel of the swatch, reach for the tape measure and the calculator and begin to plan your sweater.

MEASURING OUT YOUR DESIGN

First, write down the gauge of your swatch as so-many stitches and so-many rows to 4 in. This will be more accurate than measuring a smaller unit such as 1 in. Do the same for the row gauges.

Second, plan the size and shape of each piece you're going to knit. The easiest way to be sure that you'll get the fit you want is to measure an existing garment. Alternatively, you can take your body measurements and add movement room to suit the style of your design.

A SIMPLE SWEATER

These two variations (on diagram A) on a simple drop-sleeve sweater show how different proportions can be used to create two sweaters measuring the same from cuff to cuff.

Using the diagram on the next page as a guide, fill in your measurements. All knitting measurements should be taken with the tape measure held

> ## TIP
>
> • Experiment first with a natural-fiber yarn. Then, if you need to unravel a section of your knitting, you can simply steam out the wrinkles by holding the yarn over a recently boiled kettle and reuse the yarn. Rewind it very loosely.

straight along rows or stitches — never take it around curves or along shaped edges.

The diagram shows only half of the sleeve, so the top edge and cuff edge measurements must be doubled when calculating the width of the sleeve. For a fitted style or a shaped armhole, you'll need to take more measurements.

It's a good idea to decide on the proportions of your design by making a scale drawing on graph paper, allowing one square for each inch. This is useful if you are calculating the shape of a sleeve top in relation to the depth of an armhole, since the number of stitches and rows in the corresponding edges may vary and must be calculated separately.

If you are working out unfamiliar shapings, you could make a full-size paper pattern before you think about stitches and rows.

A

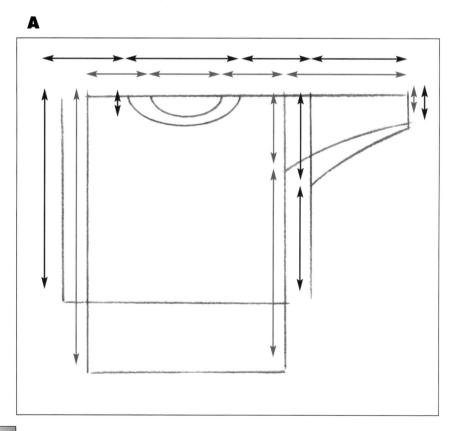

NUMBER CRUNCHING

To translate your measurements into stitches and rows, use a calculator for speed and accuracy.

PLANNING REPEATS

If you're using stockinette stitch, you can cast on the precise number of stitches needed for the width (plus two stitches that will be lost in the side seams when they are sewn up). Add or subtract a stitch or two to balance a ribbed edge. If you're using a textured stitch pattern, you will have to calculate how many multiples of the pattern—plus any edge stitches—come closest to fitting into your measurements. Check the row repeats in relation to the length in the same way.

Stockinette can be worked on any number of rows, but if working in a textured stitch, you may want to shape the shoulder or neck at the end of a pattern repeat or on a specific pattern row to avoid an ugly break. Change measurements or adapt stitch patterns until you are happy with the proportions of your design.

PLAN YOUR GARMENT

Before you measure up and plan a garment, make sure you have diagrams, swatches, and samples of yarn on hand.

• DESIGN YOUR OWN KNITS •

TIPS
FOR PROFESSIONAL RESULTS

• How many stitches to cast on for a width of 24 inches with a gauge of 5.5 stitches to one inch? 5.5 multiplied by 24 = 132 stitches.

• Calculate the number of rows to a given measurement in the same way, using the row gauge.

167

Playing with Color

INTARSIA MOTIFS

Kilims and old woven textiles are a rich source of ideas for color and patterns (right). The designs are geometric, which makes them easy to interpret on a chart.

Because kilim motifs are quite large, they specifically lend themselves to intarsia multicolor knitting. This means that you only have to establish a stockinette-stitch gauge in the yarn you want to use in order to estimate the size of your design.

Although individual motifs may be very simple in shape (below), they provide plenty of possibilities for playing with

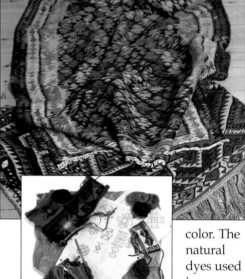

color. The natural dyes used in many antique carpets contribute to a weaving effect called "abrash," in which shades and tones of one color are mixed in an arbitrary way within a motif. Imitate this by working shaded stripes in a motif or as the background—and create an artistic effect while using up odds and ends of yarn.

SMALL REPEAT PATTERNS

If you love multicolor knitting, you'll find inspiration wherever you look. This little Buddha figure, with its patterned and plain areas, sparks off lots of color combinations for these swatches. When you choose colors, don't worry too much about matching them exactly to your inspiration. A color may look too bright on the ball, but used in tiny amounts it will wake up the softer shades. Mix in a few yarns with a slight texture to break up the regularity of the surface. Start by using the classic "two colors in a row" stranded knitting technique, then add more colors or incorporate tiny areas of intarsia. Or simply start to knit and change the colors whenever you like.

Use a chart with a small repeat, such as the

Shetland peerie patterns, and try out the effect of changing the background color and the pattern color each time to give a flickering, striped effect. The motifs don't need to be very complicated, as even the simplest little patterns come to life if you get the colors right.

```
TIP
• Color more than one repeat to
  see the effect of the pattern.
```

Adapting a Cross-Stitch Chart

*Keen color knitters are often tempted to knit from cross-stitch charts.
If you do, remember that each cross-stitch on fabric is square,
whereas each knitted stitch is a wide and short V shape.*

Light letters on a dark background emphasize the typographical effect.

With the stranded knitting technique, you may have an almost-square gauge that doesn't distort the design too much. But if you use the intarsia technique to knit directly from a cross-stitch chart, the design will be compressed vertically.

For a picture knit or a motif to be instantly recognizable—such as the letters inspired by old cross stitch samplers—you'll need to design a chart with the proportions of the gauge in mind.

The easiest way to design a chart is to work out exactly the number of stitches and rows that the motif will need in your gauge on graph paper, then fill in the design.

Designing a Motif

Charting a flower pattern is a fascinating project to take on. Choose something that's easily recognizable, such as a pansy.

Draw the flowers as accurately as you can given the limitations of the graph paper, which makes true curves difficult. Small motifs can be worked in stranded knitting.

Larger motifs or posies of flowers are best if the small areas of a particular color are intarsia-knitted and the background is stranded. Test the technique and the way the design looks by knitting swatches until you get the

desired effect. When you've designed the motif, draw a full-size

chart for the back of the garment, photocopy your motif several times, then cut out the motifs and move them around on the large chart until you achieve the desired effect.

Try designing subtle variations instead of working identical flowers.

Placing a Motif on a Simple Sweater

If you're knitting a complex motif, it's best to keep the shape of the sweater simple.

To establish your gauge, knit a swatch from part of the chart, then work out the size of the motif. Although you can add more background or frame the motif with another pattern, the size of the motif will dictate the proportions of your sweater.

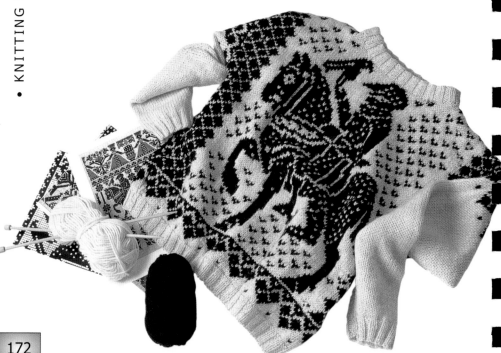

Designing a Cardigan

Scattered motifs like these floating leaves are ideal for cardigans.

All you need to do is to plan the size of the back on graph paper, then mark the position of the front edges and the shape of the neck. When placing the motifs—apparently at random—make sure that only whole motifs are on the fronts. To avoid having a band-sized gap on the back, you can make each front exactly half the width of the back.

Although bands can either be picked up or worked separately and sewn on, the smoothest bands are those knitted in with the fronts. For the bands, choose a stitch pattern with a vertical tighter gauge than that used for the main fabric—for example, garter-stitch with a stockinette main fabric. Add the number of band stitches to each front and change the stitch pattern each time you work them. Mark the buttonhole positions on your chart and work them in as you go. For a V-neck, decrease in the main stitch pattern next to the band stitches.

TIPS
FOR PROFESSIONAL RESULTS

• Make a color fringe and keep it with the chart for reference.

• Buy buttons before you make the buttonholes.

Inspiration from Contemporary Design

Fresh and full of vitality, knitting today is an eclectic mix of traditional techniques and modern style.

PINWHEEL
Eighteen colors are brilliantly combined in this exciting geometric design.

All three of the designs on these two pages are by Kaffe Fassett.

STONE CIRCLES
This design shows a
free interpretation of the
organic shapes, with
monochromatic shading.

ROSE PETALS
Ovals of color seem
to float on a neutral
background for this
neat little jacket.

Left:
Jean Moss
HAUSA JACKET
This boldly colored design is
inspired by African textiles.

Above:
Julien MacDonald
CATWALK
Anarchic student catwalk
fashion gives chunky
knitting a bold look.

Left:
Vivienne Westwood
CATWALK
The unusual combination
of a nobbly, multicolored
yarn and scaled–up
Shetland lace gives this
design great impact.

Left:
Alice Starmore
ST. BRIGID
Celtic knotwork cables are used to dramatic
effect on this fringed sweater.

Above:
Kim Hargreaves
PUNCH
Bold bands of color add emphasis to simple
stitches and a tailored shape.

Above:
Jean Moss
POOKA
Color-patterned borders and a mixture of
cables and garter stitch are used to make
this bright, button-neck sweater.

PROJECTS TO KNIT

The projects in this section are suitable for all knitting capabilities, although you may wish to add some kind of embellishment or color feature, such as beading or intarsia. Alternatively, you may decide simply to sew the pieces together in a different way than suggested by the pattern, thus creating knitted objects that are personal and unique.

All about Garments

Garments are made from shaped pieces of knitting, and now that you have learned all the skills necessary to calculate knitting patterns for any shape, writing the patterns for garments should present no difficulty, provided that you have all the necessary measurements.

Measurements for a basic round-neck sweater with set-in sleeves are given in the charts on the next page. These measurements are for a well-fitting sweater of medium length, to be worked in double-knit yarn. If the same garment were to be worked in a thicker yarn, the actual measurement would need to be more than two inches larger than the "to fit" size and all the other measurements altered in proportion. The same garment in slightly finer yarn could have less than 2 inches added to the "to fit" size. Garments always have this extra amount added to the "to fit" size unless they are meant to be very body-hugging, in which case they would probably be worked in a ribbed stitch pattern. Garments come in a variety of shapes and sizes, but they fall into five main groups:

1. SQUARE-SHAPED GARMENTS
These garments have little or no shaping.

2. GARMENTS WITH SET-IN SLEEVES
These are usually well-fitted but can have any style of neckline.

3. RAGLAN-SLEEVE GARMENTS

A raglan seam is one where the armhole seam extends from the underarm point to the neckline. Most styles of neckline can be worked with this type of garment.

4. DOLMAN-SLEEVE GARMENTS

These garments have sleeves knitted together with the body so that they have no armhole seams.

5. ROUND-YOKED GARMENTS

These garments usually have the yoke knitted in one piece with no seams. All the stitches across the sleeves and body pieces are picked up and worked for the depth of the yoke, making decreases so that it fits.

WRITING PATTERNS FOR GARMENTS

(made from squares or rectangles)
Garments can be made entirely from square or rectangular shapes. They are knitted either in one piece or in several pieces sewn together. Writing the patterns for these garments is very simple and the resulting pattern is usually very easy to knit. These simple-shaped garments are mainly used for outer garments.

A tabard is made from two rectangles sewn or tied together at the shoulders and side seams. It can also be worked in one piece with a slit like a large horizontal buttonhole, worked for the neck.

CHILDREN'S MEASUREMENTS

Age	3 yrs	6 yrs	8 yrs	10 yrs	12 yrs	14 yrs
To fit size chest	22	24	26	28	30	32 in.
Actual chest	24	26	28	29½	32	34 in.
Length from back neck	13	15	17	19¼	21½	23 in.
Armhole depth	5	6	6½	7	7½	8 in.
Back neck width	4	4½	4¾	5	5¼	5½ in.
Across chest	8½	9	9½	10	10¼	10½ in.
Sleeve seam	10¼	11	12	14½	16½	17 in.
Round top of arm	9	9¾	10	10	11	12 in.
Wrist	4	4½	4½	5	5½	6 in.

LADIES' MEASUREMENTS

To fit size bust	30	32	34	36	38	40 in.
Actual bust	32	34	36	38	40	42 in.
Length from back neck	22	23	24	25	26	26 in.
Armhole depth	7	7½	7½	8	8¼	8½ in.
Back neck width	5½	5½	6¼	6¼	7	7 in.
Across chest	11¾	12	13	13¼	14	15 in.
Sleeve seam	17	17½	17½	18	18	18½ in.
Round top of arm	11¾	13	14	14½	14¾	15 in.
Wrist	6	6½	7	7½	7¾	8¼ in.

MEN'S MEASUREMENTS

To fit chest	35½	37½	40	42	44	46 in.
Actual chest	37½	40	42	44	46	48 in.
Length from back neck	26	26	26⅜	26⅜	27½	28 in.
Armhole depth	8¼	8½	9	9½	10	11 in.
Back neck width	6¼	7	7	7½	7½	8 in.
Across chest	14	15	15¾	16½	17½	18 in.
Sleeve seam	18½	18½	19	19	19¼	19½ in.
Round top of arm	15	15¼	15¾	16	16½	17 in.
Wrist	7½	8	8¼	8½	9	9 in.

Sleeves can be added to the tabard shape by casting on extra stitches at both edges. The addition of a ribbed band worked at the cuff or hem will give the garment a better fit.

The garment can be worked in one piece, starting at the hem or the cuff, or it can be worked in several pieces, placing the seams wherever desired. The neckline can be any shape. The armhole depth needs to be deeper than that given for the set-in sleeve sweater.

Autumn in Belgravia

Brown and gray jacket with fringed shawl

GRADE ★ ★

Sizes to fit	32	34	36 in.
Actual size	42	44	46 in.
Back length	27	28	29 in.
Sleeve seam	16	16½	17 in.

MATERIALS

Jacket	12	14	16MC
	4	4	4A
Shawl	11	11	11A

x 2 oz. balls standard DK yarn

1 pr size 10 needles • 1 pr size 9 needles
• 1 pr size 8 needles • 2 large buttons
Yarn originally used: Argyll Chevalier
(using 2 ends together). Argyll Ferndale
DK.

ABBREVIATIONS

alt – alternate • beg – beginning • cont –
continue • dec – decrease • foll –
following • inc – increase • k – knit • p –
purl • patt – pattern • rem – remaining •
rep – repeat • st(s) – stitch(es) • st st –
stocking stitch • tog – together • MC –
main color • A – 1st color • B – 2nd color

TENSION
Using size 8 needles, MC over st
patt. 22 sts and 30 rows = 4 in.
square.

BACK
Using size 8 needles and MC, cast
on 119 (125; 131) sts and cont patt
as follows:
1st row: p5, * k1, p5, rep from * to
end.
2nd row: k5, * p1, k5, rep from * to
end.
Rep these 2 rows 4 more times.
11th row: p2, * k1, p5, rep from * to
last 3 sts, k1, p2.
12th row: k2, *p1, k5, rep from * to
last 3 sts, p1, k2.
Rep these last 2 rows 4 more times.
These 20 rows form the patt. Cont in
patt until work measures 11 (11¼;
12) in. Place armhole markers at
each end of last row. Cont in patt
until work measures 27 (28; 29) in.
Cast off.

POCKET BAGS
(Make 2.) Using size 8 needles and
col A, cast on 31 (32; 33) sts and
work in st st until work measures
7½ in., ending with a k row. Leave
sts on holder.

RIGHT FRONT
Using size 8 needles and MC, cast
on 65 (68; 71) sts and cont patt as
follows:
1st row: p2 (0; 2), k1 (0; 1) * p5, k1,
rep from * to last 2 sts, p2.

2nd row: k2, * p1, k5, rep from * to last 3 (0; 3) sts, p1 (0; 1), k2 (0; 2). Placement of patt is now set. Cont in patt until work measures 7½ in., ending with a wrong-side row.

PLACE POCKET
Next row: patt 17 (18; 19) sts, cast off next 31 (32; 33) sts, patt to end.
Next row: patt 17 (18; 19), patt across pocket bag, patt to end. Cont in patt to the same row as back armhole marker. Place an armhole marker at left side. Cont in patt until work measures 19 (20; 21) in., ending with a wrong-side row.

BUTTONHOLE
Next row: patt 5 sts, cast off next 3 sts, patt to end.
Next row: patt to last 5 sts, cast on 3 sts, patt to end **. Patt 28 more rows. Rep from ** to **. Cont in patt until work measures 24 (24½; 25½) in., ending with a wrong-side row.

SHAPE NECKLINE
1st row: cast off 8 (9; 19) sts, patt to end.
2nd row: patt to last 2 sts, patt 2 tog.
3rd row: cast off 5 sts, patt to end.
4th row: as 2nd row.
5th row: cast off 3 sts, patt to end. Dec 1 st at neck edge of next 5 rows. Dec 1 st at neck edge of foll 4 alt rows. Cont in patt on rem 38 (40; 42)

sts until work measures 27 (28; 29) in. Cast off.

LEFT FRONT
Work to match right front, reversing part placement and shapings and omitting buttonholes.

SLEEVES
Using size 8 needles and MC, cast on 73 (75; 77) sts and commence patt as follows.
1st row: p0 (1; 2), * k1, p5, rep from * to last 1 (2; 3) sts, k1, p0 (1; 2).
2nd row: k0 (1; 2), * p1, k5 rep from * to last 1 (2; 3) sts, p1, k0 (1; 2). Placement of patt is now set. Cont in patt and inc 1 st at each end of next and every foll alt row until there are 177 (181; 185) sts. Cont in patt without shaping until work measures 16½ (16¾; 17) in., ending with a wrong-side row. Cast off 36 sts at beg of next 4 rows. Cast off rem 33 (37; 41) sts.

SLEEVE HEM AND FACING
(Both the same.) Using size 8 needles and A, with right side facing, pick up 69 (71; 73) sts across bottom of sleeve. Work 4 rows st st beg with a p row. K1 row. Work 6 rows st st beg with a k row. Cont in st st and inc 1 st at each end of next and every foll alt row until work measures 8 in. from beg of hem. Cast off.

NECK BAND

Using small backstitch, sew both shoulder seams.

Using size 8 needles and A, with right side facing, pick 35 (37; 39) sts along right front neckline, pick up 39 (41; 43) sts across back neckline, pick up 35 (37; 39) sts along left front neckline. 109 (115; 121) sts. P1 row. Change to size 9 needles. P1 row. K1 row, decreasing 1 st at each end of row. Change to size 8 needles. P1 row. Cast off.

RIGHT FRONT HEM AND FACING

Using size 8 needles and A, with right side facing, pick up 125 (131; 137) sts along front edge. Work 4 rows st st beg with a p row and inc 1 st at each end of 2nd and 4th rows. K1 row. Work 10 rows st st, beg with a k row and decrease at each end of 1st and 3rd rows. Fold work to the inside and place marker, turn work and work 4 more rows st st on these sts. Break yarn and rejoin to rem sts. Work 5 rows st st on these sts. Cont in st st for 4 rows and inc 1 st at beg of next and foll 3rd row. Work 3 more rows st st. Cast off.

Work left front hem and facing to match, omitting buttonholes.

POCKET BANDS

(Both the same.) Using size 8 needles and A, with right side facing, pick up 27 (28; 29) sts across pocket top. K1 row. Work 2 in. st st beg with a k row. Cast off. Sew pocket flap down to outside of work.

BOTTOM HEM

Using small backstitch, sew sleeve tops into armholes between markers and sew underarm seams. Using size 8 needles and Ferndale, with right side facing, pick up 60 (62; 64) sts across left front, pick up 111 (115; 121) sts across back, pick up 60 (62; 64) sts across right front. 232 (239; 249) sts. Work 4 rows st st, beg with a p row and inc 1 st at each end of 2nd and 4th rows. K1 row. Work 4 rows st st, beg with a k row and dec 1 st at each end of 1st and 3rd rows. Cast off.

SHAWL

Using size 8 needles and A, cast on 292 sts. Work 2 rows st st, beg with a k row. (Work 3 rows st st, beg with a k row and inc 1 st at each end of every row; p1 row) x 6. Work 3 rows st st, beg with a k row and inc 1 st at each end of every row. 336 sts. K1 row. ** Work 3 rows st st, beg with a k row and dec 1 st at each end of every row. P1 row. Rep from ** until 2 sts remain. K2 tog. Fasten off. Fold in and stitch down long side facing. Cut strands of each yarn in various lengths between 16 in. and 19½ in. Fold strands in half and loop through 2 edges of shawl.

TO MAKE UP

Using small backstitch, sew the 4 front miters and sleeve seams. Fold in hems and facings and slipstitch down. Sew down pocket bags. Oversew both layers of buttonholes tog. Sew on 2 front buttons.

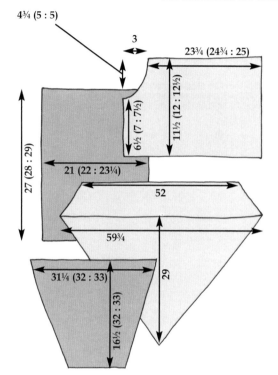

All dimensions are in inches.

4¾ (5 : 5)

3

23¾ (24¾ : 25)

11½ (12 : 12½)

6½ (7 : 7½)

27 (28 : 29)

21 (22 : 23¼)

52

59¾

31¼ (32 : 33)

29

16½ (32 : 33)

Many color combinations can be used, as shown below.

• Project 2
The Suzy Wong

Floral Chinese-style top with black buttons

GRADE

Sizes to fit	32–34	36–38 in.
Actual size	38	40 in.
Back length	21	22 in.
Sleeve seam	17	18 in.

MATERIALS

7	7	MC
3	3	A
1	1	B
1	1	C
1	1	D
2	2	E

x 2 oz. balls. Standard DK yarn
1 pr size 10 needles • 1 pr size 8
needles • 6 buttons
Yarn originally used: Argyll
Ambridge DK

ABBREVIATIONS

alt – alternate • beg – beginning
• cont – continue • dec –
decrease • foll – following • g st
– garter stitch • inc – increase •
k – knit • p – purl • patt –
pattern • rem – remainder • rep
– repeat • sts – stitch(es) • st st –
stocking stitch • tog – together •
MC – main color • A – 1st color •
B – 2nd color • C – 3rd color • D
– 4th color • E – 5th color

TENSION

Using size 8 needles over st st, 24 sts
and 32 rows = 4 in. square.

FRONT

Using size 10 needles and MC, cast
on 116 (122) sts and work ¾ in. in g
st (knit every row), ending with a
wrong-side row. Change to size 8
needles. Working in st st, foll patt
from chart.
1st row: patt 13 (1) sts, work 30 sts
of patt, rep 3 (4) times, then patt rem
13 (1) sts.
　When work measures 12 in.
from beg, ending with a wrong-side
row, mark each end of last row to
indicate start of armholes. When
work measures 21 (22) in. from beg,
cast off.

TIP
FOR A PROFESSIONAL RESULT

• When working a color pattern,
the yarns must be woven in very
loosely across the back of the
work so that the tension is not
affected and the weaving in
should not be noticeable from
the right side.

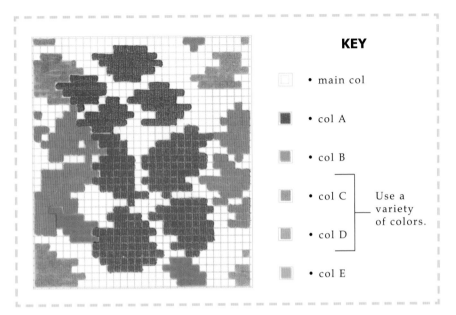

KEY

- main col
- col A
- col B
- col C ⎤
- col D ⎦ Use a variety of colors.
- col E

RIGHT HALF OF BACK

Using size 10 needles and MC, cast on 60 (62) sts and work 1 in. in g st, ending with a wrong-side row.

Change to size 8 needles. Foll patt from chart.

1st row: patt 0 (1) sts, work 30 sts of patt, rep twice, then patt rem 0 (1) sts. When work measures 12 in. from beg, mark armholes. When work measures 21 (22) in. from beg, cast off.

LEFT HALF OF BACK

Work as given for right half of back until the 1st 2 (4) rows of chart have been worked. Make buttonhole.

1st row: patt 2 sts, cast off 3 sts, patt 55 (57) sts to end.

2nd row: patt 55 (57) sts, cast on 3 sts, patt to end.

Cont as given for left half of back, making 5 more buttonholes over the previous buttonhole, working 24 rows between each buttonhole. Work to end. Cast off.

SLEEVES

Using size 10 needles and MC, cast on 60 (62) sts and work 1 in. in g st, ending with a wrong-side row.

Change to size 8 needles. Work in patt from chart as given for 1st patt row of back. And inc 1 st at each end of every 4th row, incorporating the sts into the patt until there are 116 (126) sts. Cont straight until work measures 17 (18) in. from beg. Cast off.

COLLAR

Using small backstitch, join 4½ (4¾) in. of both shoulder seams. Using size 10 needles and MC, with right side of work facing, pick up and knit 36 (34) sts from left half of back, 64 (62) sts from front, and 36 (34) sts from right half of back. 136 (130) sts. Work 4½ in. in g st. Cast off loosely. Fold neck band in half to outside.

BACK EDGINGS

Using size 10 needles and MC, pick up and knit 130 (134) sts along center back edges. Cast off knitwise.

TO MAKE UP

Using small backstitch, set in sleeves matching sleeve side seam with start of armholes. Join side and sleeve seams. Sew on buttons.

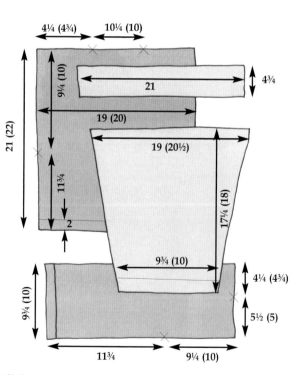

4¼ (4¾)   10¼ (10)

9¼ (10)

21

19 (20)

19 (20½)

4¾

21 (22)

11¾

2

17¼ (18)

9¾ (10)

9¾ (10)

11¾

9¼ (10)

4¼ (4¾)

5½ (5)

All dimensions are in inches.

- Project 3
Tile Style

Men's patchwork-style sweater

GRADE ★ ★ ★ ★

Sizes to fit	36–40 in.
Actual size	44 in.
Back length	28 in.
Sleeve seam	17 in.

MATERIALS

13 x 2 oz. balls standard DK yarn
• 1 pr size 10 needles • 1 pr size 8
needles • 3 buttons

ABBREVIATIONS

alt – alternate • beg – beginning
• cont – continue • dec –
decrease • foll – following • inc –
increase • k – knit • p – purl •
patt – pattern • rem – remaining
• rep – repeat • st(s) – stitch(es)
• st st – stocking stitch • tog –
together

TENSION

Using size 8 needles over moss rib
for square A, 24 sts and 32 rows =
4 in. square. Using size 8 needles,
over cable patt for square B, 33 sts
and 32 rows = 4 in.

SQUARE A

Worked over 19 sts.
1st row: k 19.
2nd row: p2, (k1, p1) 5, 8, p1.
Rep rows 1 & 2 12 more times:
(26 rows).

SQUARE B

Worked over 26 sts.
1st row: right side: (p2, k1) x 4, p2.
2nd row: (k2, p4) x 4, k2.
Rep rows 1 & 2 once more.
5th row: (p2, k4) x 4, p2.
6th row: as 2nd row.
Rep 1st 2 rows once more.
Rep rows 3–8 twice more (26 rows).

BACK

Using size 10 needles, cast on 123 sts
and work in single rib as follows:
1st row: k2, * p1, k1, rep from * to
last st, k1.
2nd row: k1, * p1, k1, rep from * to
end.
   Rep these 2 rows until work
measures 2½ in., ending with a 1st
row and inc 1 st in the last st
worked (124 sts).
Next row: rib 2, *rib 1, inc in next st,
rib 2, rep from * to last 2 sts, rib to
end, (154 sts).
   Change to size 8 needles and cont

in patt as follows:

Work rows 1–26 of the patt squares A & B, alternating them and starting with a square A.

27th–29th rows: Work in reverse st st.

30th row: * k3, (inc in next st, k1) x 7, k5, (k2 tog, k1) x 7, rep from * to last 19 sts, k3, (inc in next st, k1) x 7, k2, (161 sts).

Now work rows 1–26 of the patt squares A & B, alternating them and starting with a square B.

57th–59th rows: Work in reverse st st.

60th row: * k3, (k2 tog, k1) x 7, k5, (inc in next st, k1) x 7, k2, rep from * to last 26 sts, k3 (k2 tog, k1) x 7, k2 (154 sts).

These 60 rows form the patt. Cont in patt until work measures 28 in., ending with a 57th patt row. Cast off on next row.

Place neckline marker each side of the center 53 sts.

FRONT

Using size 10 needles, cast on 123 sts and work in single rib as given for the back (for 2¾ in., ending with a 1st row).

Next row: rib 4 * rib 1, inc 1 next st, rib 1, rep from * to last 5 sts, rib to end (161 sts).

Change to size 8 needles and cont in patt, starting with row 3. Shape neckline when work measures approximately 20 in., ending with a 28th patt row.

SHAPING NECKLINE

Patt across next row and cast off center 26 sts. Work on the last group of sts only as follows:

** Cont in patt and dec 1 st at neck edge of every foll 3rd row until 17 sts have been decreased in this manner, then cont without shaping until work measures same as back to shoulders, ending with the same patt row. Cast off.

Rejoin yarn to rem sts and work 2nd side of neck to match 1st side as given from **.

SLEEVES

Using size 10 needles, cast on 55 sts and work in single rib as given for the back for 5½ in., ending with a 1st row.

Change to size 8 needles and work in patt as given for the back, starting with a square A. At the same time inc 1 st at each end of every foll 5th row and incorporate the sts into the patt. Continue in this manner until one extra pattern square has been increased at each side of work. Cont in patt without shaping until work measures approximately 20 in., ending with a 59th patt row. Work 2 more rows in reverse st st. Cast off loosely.

COLLAR

Using size 10 needles, cast on 15 sts and work in single rib as given for the back, for 4 rows.

BUTTONHOLES

* Rib 1st 4 sts of next row, turn and work 2 more rows on these sts, break yarn and rejoin to rem sts. Work 3 rows on these sts. Work 6 rows across all the sts. Rep from * once more, then work 1 more buttonhole. At the same time, inc 1 st at the left-hand edge of the work on every 3rd row from the beg, 19 times in all, then cont in rib for another 54 rows. Now dec 1 st at left edge of every 3rd row 19 times in all. Cast off ribwise.

TO MAKE UP

Using small backstitch, sew shoulder seams. Sew sleeves to armholes, matching patt squares as far as possible. Sew 1st 2¾ in. of cuff on right side, then sew underarm seam from cuff to hem on inside. Sew shaped edge of collar to neckline, with buttons on left side. Sew cast-on and cast-off edges of collar to cast-off stitches at center front so that they overlap with button edge at front. Sew button into place.

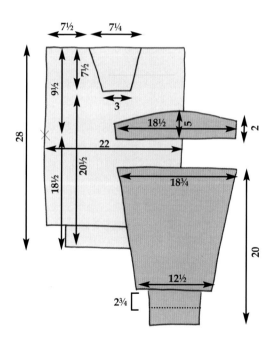

All dimensions are in inches.

• Project 4

Amazing Lace

Two-color lacy cardigan with maze pattern

GRADE

Sizes to fit	34–38 in.
Actual size	42 in.
Back length	25 in.
Sleeve seam	17 in.

MATERIALS

10 MC/8 A
x 2 oz. balls Standard DK yarn
1 pr size 10 needles • 1 pr size 8
needles • 1 circular size 10
needle • 5 buttons
Yarn originally used: Pingouin Fil
D'Ecosse No. 3

ABBREVIATIONS

alt – alternate • beg – beginning
• cont – continue • dec –
decrease • foll – following • inc –
increase • k – knit • p – purl •
patt – pattern • rem – remaining
• rep – repeat • sl – slip • st(s) –
stitch(es) • st st – stocking stitch
• tog – together • MC – main
color • A – 1st color

TENSION
Using size 8 needles over st, patt
22 sts and 46 rows = 4 in. square.

BACK
Using size 10 needles and MC, cast
on 118 sts and work in double rib as
follows:
1st row: k2, * p2, k2, rep from * to
end.
2nd row: p2, * k2, p2, rep from * to
end.
Rep these 2 rows 3 more times
and dec 1 st in last st worked. 117
sts.
Change to size 8 needles and cont
in patt from the chart, the 1st row
being:
1st chart row: using col A, k3, * sl 1,
k1, sl1, k 17, sl1, k1, rep from * to
last 4 sts, sl1, k3.
Cont in patt until work measures
14½ in., place armhole marker at
each end of this last row, then cont
in patt until work measures 25 in.,
ending with a wrong-side row.

SHAPE SHOULDERS
Cast off 19 sts at beg of next 2 rows.
Cast off 18 sts at beg of foll 2 rows.
Cast off rem 43 sts.

POCKET BAGS
(Make 2.) Using size 8 needles and
MC, cast on 31 sts and work in st st
for 4½ in. Leave sts on stitch holder.

LEFT FRONT

Using size 10 needles and MC, cast on 58 sts and work in double rib as given for the back for 8 rows, and inc 1 st in last st worked, 59 sts.

Change to size 8 needles and cont in patt from the chart, the 1st row being:

1st chart row: using A, k3, * sl1, k1, sl1, k17, sl1, k1, rep from * to last 12 sts, sl1, k1, sl1, k9.

Cont in patt until work measures 5 in., ending with a wrong-side row.

PLACE POCKET

Next row: patt 14 sts, cast off 31 sts, patt rem 14 sts.
Next row: patt 14 sts, with wrong side of pocket bag facing, patt across 31 sts of pocket bag, patt rem 14 sts.

Cont in patt until work measures 14½ in., ending with a right-side row at the center front edge.

Place an armhole marker at beg of this last row.

SHAPE NECKLINE

Cont in patt and dec 1 st at beg of next row, and at neck edge only of every foll 5th row until 22 sts have been decreased in all, then cont without shaping until work measures 24½ in., ending at armhole edge.

METHOD OF WORKING THE CHART

Alternate col A and MC, working two rows of each throughout the pattern, each time working from the chart only in that color shown. Slip all remaining stitches with yarn at back on right-side rows, and yarn at front on wrong-side rows. Work every row as a knit row.

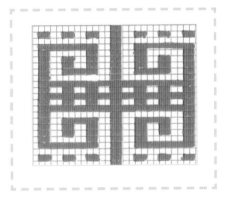

SHAPE SHOULDERS

Cast off 19 sts at beg of next row, and 18 sts at beg of foll alt row.

RIGHT FRONT

Work as given for left front, reversing shaping and pattern, the 1st chart row of pattern being:
1st row: using A, k9, sl1, k1, * sl1, k1, sl1, k17, sl1, k1, rep from to last 4 sts, sl1, k3.

SLEEVES

Using size 10 needles and MC, cast on 58 sts and work in double rib as given for the back, for 8 rows and inc 1 st in last st worked (59 sts).

Change to size 8 needles and cont in patt from the chart, the 1st row being:

1st chart row: using A, k5, sl1, k1, * sl1, k1, sl1, k17, sl1, k1, rep from * to last 8 sts, sl1, k1, sl1, k5.

Cont in patt and inc 1 st at each end of every foll 6th row until there are 115 sts, then cont without shaping until work measures 17 in.

SHAPE SLEEVE TOPS
Cont in patt and cast off 23 sts at beg of next 5 rows. Fasten off. Work second sleeve to match.

NECK BAND
Using small backstitch, sew both shoulder seams. Using long size 10 circular needle and working from the right side, pick up 82 sts between lower edge of right front and beg of neck shaping, pick up 158 sts around neckline to end of left front neck shaping, pick up 82 sts between this point and lower edge of left front, 322 sts.

Working in rows, work in double rib as given for the back, starting with a 2nd row, for 3 rows.

Next row: rib 3 sts, * cast off 3 sts, rib 16 rep from * 3 more times, cast off 3 sts, rib to end of row.

Next row: working rib, casting on 3 sts over each group of cast-off sts. Work for 2 more rows in rib. Cast off ribwise on next row.

POCKET TOPS
(Make 2.) Using size 10 needles and MC, pick up 30 sts from right side of pocket top and work in double rib for 7 rows. Cast off ribwise on next row.

TO MAKE UP
Using small backstitch, sew sleeves into armholes between markers, sew underarm seam from wrist to hem, sew pocket bags to inside front, sew buttons into place.

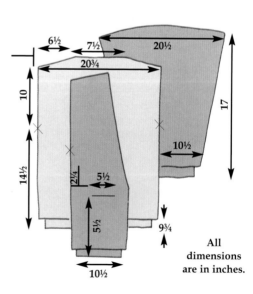

6½   7½   20½
20¾
10
17
10½
14½   2¼   5½
5½
9¾
10½

All dimensions are in inches.

Man's Sweater with Zipper

This is a variation on the sweater with seed stitch borders. A pouch pocket has been added, as well as a hem to the bottom edge and cuffs. A zipper is used on the neckline, and knitted cord gives the appearance of cable work on the sleeves and pocket edge.

GRADE

To fit chest

| 40 in. | 42 in. | 44 in. |

Actual Measurements

Chest

| 50 in. | 52 in. | 54 in. |

Length to Shoulder

| 24¾ in. | 25½ in. | 26½ in. |

Sleeve Length

| 21 in. | 21¼ in. | 22 in. |

MATERIALS

22 (23; 24) x 2 oz. Jaeger Matchmaker merino aran in shade 754.

1 pair each size 8 and size 7 needles
Set of four double-pointed size 8 needles

4 in. zipper

ABBREVIATIONS

alt – alternate • beg – beginning • cont – continue • dec – decrease • foll – following • inc – increase • k – knit • p – purl • patt – pattern • rem – remaining • rep – repeat • sl – slip • st(s) – stitch(es) • st st – stocking stitch

BACK

With size 8 needles, cast on 122 (128; 134) sts.
Beg with a k row, cont in st st for 15 rows.
Next row (fold line to form hemline): k to end.
Change to size 7 needles. Beg with a k row, cont in st st until back measures 23 (24; 24) in. from hemline, ending with a p row.

TO SHAPE NECK

Next row: k44 (46; 48) sts, turn and work on these sts for first side of neck.
Dec 1 st at neck edge on next 4 rows.
Work 1 row.

TO SHAPE SHOULDER

Bind off 20 (21; 22) sts at beg of next row.
Work 1 row.
Bind off rem 20 (21; 22) sts.
With right side facing, slip next 34 (36; 38) sts on a spare needle, rejoin yarn to next st, k to end.
Complete to match first side.

POCKET LINING

With size 8 needles, cast on 48 (50; 52) sts.
Starting with a k row, work 16 rows in st st.
Leave these sts on a spare needle.

FRONT

With size 8 needles, cast on 122 (128; 134) sts.
Beg with a k row, cont in st st for 15 rows.

Next row (fold line to make hemline): K to end.

Change to size 7 needles. Beg with a k row, work 32 rows in st st.

PLACE POCKET

Next row: k37 (39; 41) sts, leave these sts on a holder, k next 48 (50; 52) sts, turn and leave rem 37 (39; 41) sts on a holder.
Starting with a p row, work 45 rows on 48 (50; 52) sts, leave these sts on a holder.

With right side facing, slip sts on left-hand side of front onto a needle, k across sts of pocket lining, then k37 (39; 41) sts on right-hand side of front, 122 (127; 132) sts.

Starting with a p row, work 45 rows.

Next row: With right side facing, k37 (39; 41) sts, with pocket lining behind front, (k next st on front tog with next st on pocket lining) 48 (50; 52) times, k37 (39; 41). 122 (127; 132) sts.
Starting with a p row, cont in st st until front measures 21½ (22½; 23) in. from hemline, ending with a p row.

TO SHAPE NECK

Next row: k49 (51; 53) sts, turn and work on these sts for first side of neck.
Dec 1 st at neck edge on every foll alt row until 40 (42; 44) sts rem.
Cont straight until front measures same as back to shoulder, ending at side edge.

TO SHAPE SHOULDER

Bind off 20 (21; 22) sts at beg of next row.
Work 1 row.
Bind off rem 20 (21; 22) sts.
With right side facing, slip center 24 (26; 28) sts onto a holder, rejoin yarn to rem sts, k to end.
Complete to match first side.

SLEEVES

With size 8 needles, cast on 40 (42; 44) sts.
Beg with a k row, cont in st st for 15 rows.

Next row (fold line to form hemline): k to end.
Change to size 7 needles.
Beg with a k row, cont in st st.
Work 20 rows.

Next row (inc row): k3, m1, k to last 3 sts, m1, k3.
Work 3 rows.
Rep the last 4 rows until there are 92 (94; 96) sts.
Work straight until sleeve measures 21 (21½; 22) in. from hemline, ending with a p row.
Bind off.

NECK BAND

Join shoulder seams.
With set of size 8 double-pointed needles and right side facing, slip first 12 (13; 14) sts from front neck onto a needle, join on yarn, pick up and k15 sts up right side of front neck, pick up and k15 sts down left side of front neck, k across first 12 (13; 14) sts from front neck holder.

Arrange sts evenly on three needles and work backward and forward in rows.
Next row: k1, p to last st, k1.
Next row: k to end.
Rep the last 2 rows until neck band measures 4 in., ending with a right-side row.
Knit 1 row to form hemline.
Next row: k1, p to last st, k1.
Next row: k to end.
Rep last 2 rows until neck band measures 4 in. from fold line, ending with a wrong-side row.
Bind off.

CORDS

(Make 2.) With two double-pointed size 8 needles, cast on 4 sts.
K1 row, do not turn * now bring yarn tightly across the back of the work, k4 rep from * until cord measures 39 in. Fasten off.
Make two more cords 6 in. long.

TO FINISH

With center of sleeve to shoulder seam, sew on sleeves. Join side and sleeve seams. Sew down pocket lining. Sew in zipper. Pin and sew cords in place.

• Project 6
Child's Sweater

This chunky sweater is styled very simply with drop shoulders and no armhole shaping, so you can concentrate on the intarsia rabbit motif. The eyes, nose, and whiskers are embroidered after knitting is complete, and a pom-pom tail added to complete the picture.

GRADE

To fit chest

| 20 | 22 | 24 | 26 in. |

Actual measurement

| 23 | 25 | 27½ | 29½ in. |

Length to shoulder

| 12½ | 13¼ | 16 | 18 in. |

Sleeve seam

| 8 | 9¼ | 11½ | 13 in. |

MATERIALS

Sirdar Snuggly Chunky (approx. 80 yds. per 2 oz. ball)

Color A, bluebell (shade 354) 4 (5; 6; 7) 2 oz. balls

Color B, white (shade 251) 1 (1; 1; 1)

Color C, small amount of dark gray yarn for embroidery

Needles, sizes 9 and 10½

Set of 4 double-pointed needles or short circular needles, sizes 9 and 10½

2 stitch holders

ABBREVIATIONS

k – knit • p – purl • rep – repeat • st(s) – stitches • inc – increase • m1 tbl – make 1 through back loop • k2tog – knit two together • SKP – slip one, knit one pass slip stitch over • p2tog – purl two together • p2tog tbl – purl 2 together through back loops • col – color • in. – inches • beg – beginning• foll – following

GAUGE

Required gauge over stockinette is 14 sts and 19 rows to 4 in. Using size 10 needles, cast on 20 sts and work 24 rows stockinette. Measure gauge. If your gauge is tight, with more sts or rows to 4 in., try another test-piece with larger needles. If your gauge is loose, with fewer sts or rows to 4 in., try again with smaller needles.

BACK

Using size 9 needles and col A, cast on 42 (46; 50; 54) sts.
Row 1: * k1, p1, rep from * to end.
Rep this row 3 (5; 5; 5) more times.
4 (6; 6; 6) rib rows in all.
Change to size 10½ needles. *
Row 1: k to end.

Row 2: k1, p to last st, k1. Work all wrong-side rows of stockinette in this way, with 1 selvage st at each edge.

Rep these 2 rows, 13 (16; 20; 24) more times. 28 (34; 42; 50) rows of stockinette in all, ending with a p row.

Place a marker at each end of last row. These mark the beg of the armhole.

Rep rows 1 and 2, 13 (13; 14; 15) more times. 26 (26; 28; 30) rows in all from markers, ending with a p row. 54 (60; 70; 80) stockinette rows in all.

SHAPE SHOULDERS

Bind off 6 (6; 7; 7) sts at beg next 2 rows, knitwise on k row, purlwise on p row.

Bind off 6 (7; 7; 8) sts at beg foll 2 rows. 18 (20; 22; 24) sts remain. Slip these sts onto a stitch holder and cut yarn, leaving a 6 in. tail.

TIP

• Choose a finer yarn for the embroidery, such as DK or worsted weight. Use it double for the swiss darning, to cover the stitches well. And use it singly for the whiskers so they are not too clumsy.

FRONT

Work as given for back to **. Work in stockinette as given for back for 0 (6; 10; 14) rows, thus ending with a wrong-side row. (NOTE: for 1st size only, motif begins immediately after rib rows.)

RABBIT MOTIF

(See chart on next page.) From a new ball of col A, wind off about 4 yds. into a small ball. From the ball of col B, wind off about 5 yds. into a small ball.

These balls will be used later when working the two ears. Read right-side (k) rows (odd numbers) from right to left, and wrong-side (p) rows from left to right.

Chart row 1: With ball of col A already in use, k10 (12; 14; 16) sts, using large ball of col B, k18 sts, using new ball of col A, k14 (16; 18; 20) sts to end.

Chart row 2: Using col A, k1, p13 (15; 17; 19), change to col B, p19 sts, change to col A, p8 (10; 12; 14), k1. Continue in this way, reading from successive chart rows, keeping motif correct.

On chart row 15: Under rabbit's front leg, carry col A across back of 7 sts, twisting yarns twice to prevent a long "float."
When chart row 28 (28; 32; 36) is complete, place a marker at each end of last row.

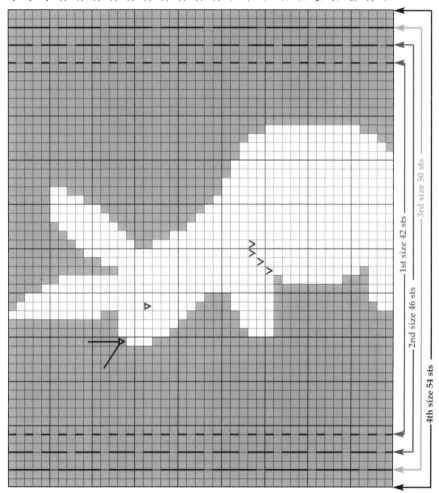

KEY

• Swiss darn in color A

• Swiss darn in color C

• Straight stitches in color C

On chart row 33: Use ball of col B already in work for sts of first ear, join in small ball of col A for sts between ears, and join in small ball of col B for sts of second ear. Continue until chart row 45 is complete.

Change to col A and stockinette, beg with a p row work 1 (1; 5; 11) rows, 46 (52; 60; 70) rows in all from last rib row.

SHAPE FRONT NECK: first side
1st neck row: k17 (18; 20; 21) sts, turn. Work on these sts only.
2nd neck row: p2tog, p to last st, k1.
3rd neck row: k to last 2 sts, k2tog.
Rep 2nd and 3rd neck rows 1 (1; 2; 2) more times.
1st and 2nd sizes only: Work 2nd neck row once again.

ALL SIZES
12 (13; 14; 15) sts remain. Work 2 (2; 3; 3) more rows, ending p row. 54 (60; 70; 80) rows in all from last rib row, matching. Back at beg of shoulder shaping.

SHAPE SHOULDER
Next row: Bind off 6 (6; 7; 7) sts knitwise, k to end.
Following row: p to end.
Bind off remaining 6 (7; 7; 8) sts knitwise. Cut yarn, leaving a 12 in. tail.

SHAPE FRONT NECK: second side
With right side of front facing, slip 8 (10; 10; 12) sts at center onto a stitch holder and rejoin col A at right of remaining 17 (18; 20; 21) sts.
1st neck row: k to end.
2nd neck row: p to last 2 sts, p2tog tbl.
3rd neck row: SKP, k to end.
Rep 2nd and 3rd next rows, 1 (1; 2; 2) more times.
1st and 2nd sizes only: Work 2nd neck row once again.

SHAPE SHOULDER
Next row: Bind off 6 (6; 7; 7) sts purlwise, p to end.
Following row: k to end.
Bind off remaining 6 (7; 7; 8) sts purlwise. Cut yarn, leaving a 12 in. tail.

SLEEVE (make 2)
Using size 9 needles and col A, cast on 26 (26; 28; 28) sts.
Row 1: *k1, p1, rep from * to end.
Rep this row 5 more times, 6 rib rows in all.
Change to size 10½ needles.

SHAPE SLEEVE
Inc row 1: k1, m1 tbl, k to last st, m1 tbl, k1. 28 (28; 30; 30) sts.
Work 5 rows stockinette, beginning and ending p row with selvage sts, as for back.
Rep these 6 rows, 3 (5; 5; 6) more times. 34 (38; 40; 42) sts. 24 (36; 36;

42) rows of stockinette in all from last rib row.

Work in row 1 again. 36 (40; 42; 44) sts.

Continue in stockinette, beginning p row until sleeve measures 8 (9¼; 11½; 13) in. in all from cast-on edge, or length required, ending with a p row.

Bind off loosely.

ASSEMBLY

Run in all yarn ends from motif.

Work embroidery on motif as shown on chart. Join shoulder seams with backstitch, using ends left for this purpose. Fold one sleeve in half lengthwise to find center of top edge. Match this point to shoulder seam. Match top corners of sleeve to markers on side edges of back and front. Join armhole seam. Join top edge of other sleeve to armhole in same way. Join side and sleeve seams using mattress stitch, taking selvage sts into seams.

CREW NECK

With right side of work facing, using set of 4 double-pointed needles or circular size 9 needles and col A, begin at right shoulder seam; k across 18 (20; 22; 24) sts from holder at back neck; pick up and k10 (10; 11; 11) sts from first side of front neck

shaping; k across 8 (10; 10; 12) sts from holder at center front and pick up and k10 (10; 11; 11) sts from second side of front neck shaping. 46 (50; 54; 58) sts.

Round 1: *k1, p1, rep from * to end. Rep this round 3 more times.

Change to a size 10½ needle and bind off in k and p as established.

Using col B, make a pom-pom (see page 51) about 2 in. across. Sew in place for rabbit's tail. Run in any remaining yarn ends along seams.

• Project 7
The Silver Lining

The sun breaks through a cloudy sky on this mohair jacket.

209

GRADE ★ ★ ★ ★

Sizes to fit	32–34	36–38 in.
Actual size	40	44 in.
Back length	24	25 in.
Sleeve seam	17	18 in.

MATERIALS

13	13	MC
9	10	A
2	3	B

x 1 oz. ball mohair thick yarn
• Needles, sizes 5 and 7
• 1 button

Yarn originally used: Sirdar Nocturne

ABBREVIATIONS

alt – alternate • beg – beginning • cont – continue • dec – decrease • foll – following • inc – increase • k – knit • p – purl • patt – pattern • rem – remaining • rep – repeat • st(s) – stitch(es) • st st – stocking stitch • tog – together • MC – main color • A – 1st color • B – 2nd color

TENSION
Using size 5 needles over patt 16 sts and 21 rows of 4 in. square.

NOTE
When working the color pattern, the yarns must be woven in very loosely across the back of the work so that the tension is not affected and the weaving in should not be noticeable from the right side.

POCKET BAGS (make 2)
Using size 5 needles and MC, cast on 28 sts and work in st st for 5½ in., leave on a stitch holder.

BACK & FRONT (worked in one)
Using size 5 needles and MC, cast on 162 (180) sts and work in color patt from the chart as follows:
1st row: *k6MC, k4A, k8MC, rep from * to end. Cont in color patt from the chart and inc 1 st at each end of every foll 7th row (incorporating these extra sts into color patt). At the same time, when work measures 6 in., ending with a wrong side row, place pockets.

POCKETS (make 2)
Patt across 8 sts, cast off next 28 sts, patt across rem sts to last 36 sts.

Cast off next 28 sts, patt rem 8 sts.
Next row: patt across 8 sts, patt across top of pocket, patt to last 36 sts, patt across top of next pocket bag, patt rem 8 sts.

Cont in patt, working shaping on these sts until work measures 14 (14½) in., ending with a wrong-side row.

DIVIDE FOR ARMHOLES
Divide work into 3 sections with 87 (90) sts in the middle back section. Work on left front only as follows: **Cont to inc at front edge only, as before, until 16 increases have been worked in all, then cont without shaping until work measures 22 (23½) in., ending at front edge.

SHAPE NECKLINE
Cast off 20 sts, patt to end.
Next row: patt to last 2 sts, p2tog.
Next row: cast off 4 sts, patt to end. Now dec 1 st at neck edge only of next 7 (6) rows, then cont in patt on rem 25 (30) sts until work measures 24 (25) in. Cast off.

Rejoin yarn to right front and work to match left front. At the same time, work buttonhole, 2 rows below beg of neck shaping, by casting off 3 sts, 2 sts in from the edge on the next row, and then casting these 3 sts on over the cast-off sts on foll row.

Rejoin yarn to 80 (90) sts for back and work in patt until work measures 24 (25) in. Cast off.

SLEEVES
Using size 5 needles and MC, cast on 54 sts and work in patt, the 1st row being as for the back. At the same time, inc 1 st at each end of every foll 7th (5th) row until there are 78 (86) sts, then cont without shaping until work measures 16¾ (17) in. Cast off.

HEM EDGING
Using size 7 needles and working from the right side using B, pick up 174 (192) sts evenly around hem. Cast off knitwise on next row.

FRONT EDGES
Using size 7 needles and B, pick up 92 (96) sts from right side of front edge. Cast off knitwise on next row.

NECK EDGE
Using small backstitch, sew shoulder seams. Using size 7 needles and B, pick up 76 (80) sts from right side of neck edge. Cast off knitwise on next row.

SLEEVE EDGE
Using size 7 needles and B, and working from right side, pick up 56 sts evenly along lower edge of sleeve. Cast off knitwise on next row.

POCKET EDGE
Using size 7 needles and B, pick up 30 sts from right side of pocket top. Cast off knitwise on next row.

TO MAKE UP

Using small backstitch, sew sleeve seams, sew sleeves into armholes, and sew pocket bags to inside. Sew button in place. Using B, work French knots at random over garment.

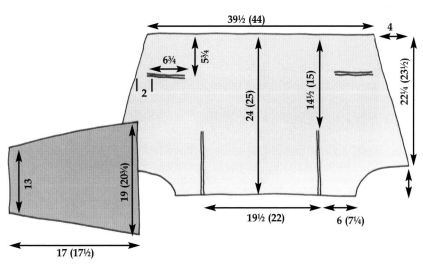

39½ (44)

4

6¾

5¾

2

24 (25)

14½ (15)

22¼ (23½)

13

19 (20¾)

19½ (22)

6 (7¼)

17 (17½)

All dimensions are in inches.

Project 8
Winter Sweater

Child's multicolored sweater

GRADE

	Sizes to fit		
24	26	28	30 in.

	Actual size		
26	28	30	32 in.

	Back length		
15	16½	18	20 in.

	Sleeve seam		
11	12	14½	16 in.

MATERIALS

3	3	4	4 A
2	2	2	3 B
2	2	2	3 C
2	2	2	3 D

x 2 oz. balls standard DK yarn

1 pr size 9 needles • 1 pr size 11 needles • 1 x 4 (4; 4; 6) in. zipper

Yarn originally used: Pingouin Pingofrance

ABBREVIATIONS

alt – alternate • beg – beginning • cont – continue • dec – decrease • foll – following • inc – increase • k – knit • p – purl • patt – pattern • rem – remaining • rep – repeat • st(s) – stitch(es) • st st – stocking stitch • tog – together • A – 1st color • B – 2nd color • C – 3rd color • D – 4th color

TENSION
Using size 9 needles over st st, 23 sts and 30 rows = 4 in. square.

BACK
Using size 11 needles and A, cast on 62 (70; 78; 90) sts.
1st row: *k2, p2, rep from * to last 2 sts, k2.
2nd row: *p2, k2, rep from * to last 2 sts, p2.
Rep these 2 rows until work measures 2 in., ending with a 1st row.
Next row: rib 3 (4; 6; 4), [inc in next st, rib 4 (4; 4; 7)] x 11 (12; 13; 10), inc in next st, rib to end. 74 (83; 92; 101) sts.
    Change to size 9 needles and cont in st patt as follows:
1st row: k1B, * k8B, k1C, rep from * to last st, k1C.
2nd row: p1C, * p2C, p7B, rep from * to last st, p1B.

3rd row: k1B, * k6B, k3C, rep from * to last st, k1C.

4th row: p1C, *p4C, p5B, rep from * to last st, p1B.

5th row: k1B, * k4B, k5C, rep from * to last st, k1C.

6th row: p1C, p3B, rep from * to last st, k1C.

7th row: k1B, * k2B, k7C, rep from * to last st, k1C.

8th row: p1C, * p8C, p1B, rep from * to last st, p1B.

9th row: k1A, * k8A, k1D, rep from * to last st, k1D.

10th row: p1D, * p2D, p7A, rep from * to last st, p1A.

11th row: k1A, * k6A, k3D, rep from * to last st, k1D.

12th row: p1D, * p4D, p5A, rep from * to last st, p1A.

13th row: k1A, * k4A, k5D, rep from * to last st, k1D.

14th row: p1D, *p6D, p3A, rep from * to last st, p1A.

15th row: k1A, * k2A, k7D, rep from * to last st, k1D.

16th row: p1D, *p8D, p1A, rep from * to last st, p1A.

These 16 rows form the patt. Cont in patt until work measures 10 (10½; 12; 13) in. from beg. Place armhole markers at each end of the last row and cont in patt until work measures 15 (16½; 18; 20) in. from beg. Cast off, placing each neckline marker in sts 25 (28; 31; 34) and sts 50 (56; 62; 68).

FRONT

Work as given for the back until work measures 10 (10½; 12; 13) in. from beg, ending with a right-side row.

SHAPE NECKLINE

Next row: 1st and 3rd sizes only, patt 37 (46) sts, turn, 2nd and 4th sizes only patt 40 (49) sts, patt 2 tog, turn.

*Cont on these 37 (41; 46; 50) sts in patt and dec 1 st at neck edge of the next and every foll 3rd row until 24 (27; 30; 33) sts remain. Cont in patt without shaping to same patt row as the back at casting off. Cast off.

Rejoin the yarn to rem sts and rep from * to *.

SLEEVES

Using size 11 needles and A, cast on 30 (30; 34; 34) sts and working double rib as given for the back, beg with a 2nd row until work measures 4½ in., ending with a 1st row.

Next row: rib 0 (0; 3; 3), [inc in next st, rib 3 (3; 2; 2)] x 7 (7; 9; 9), inc in next st, rib to end. 38 (38; 44; 44) sts.

Change to size 9 needles and commence st patt as follows:

1st row: k1 (1; 4; 4) B, * k8C, k1B, rep from * to last 1 (1; 4; 4) sts, k1 (1; 4; 4) C. The position of the st patt is now set. Cont in patt and inc 1 st at each end of every foll 4th (4th;

5th; 5th) row until there are 66 (70; 74; 78) sts. Cont in patt without shaping until work measures 13 (14; 17; 18) in. from beg. Cast off.

COLLAR

Using size 11 needles and A, cast on 94 (98; 102; 110) sts and work in double rib as given for the back and dec 1 st at each end of the 2nd and every foll alt row until 72 (74; 78; 86) sts remain.

Cont in rib without shaping until work measures 4 in.

Next row: rib 23 (23; 23; 26) sts, cast off 26 (28; 32; 34) sts, rib to end. Cont in rib on last group of 23 (23; 23; 26) sts only as follows:

Next row: rib to last 2 sts, rib 2tog.

Cont in rib and dec 1 st at the same edge as the 1st dec on every foll 2nd (2nd; 2nd; 3rd) row until 1 st remains. Fasten off. Rejoin yarn to rem 23 (23; 23; 26) sts and work to match the 1st side, reversing shaping.

TO MAKE UP

Using small backstitch, sew shoulder seams, sew sleeve tops into armholes, and sew side and sleeve seams. Pin the collar neatly around the neckline and stitch in place. Sew zipper into front opening of collar.

All dimensions are in inches.

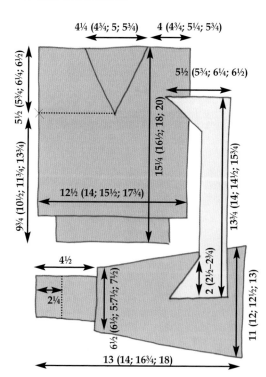

Small Shoulder Bag with Flap Detail

This is a simple pattern to follow and is designed with the novice knitter in mind. The bag itself is stockinette stitch with a twisted cord strap and a knitted flap. Knitting a bag or purse was a favorite pastime at the turn of the last century. Made using fine yarns, color, and beads, these simple purses are based on a knitted rectangle, giving you three alternative design options.

GRADE

Measurements
5 in. wide by 7 in. long

Gauge
28 sts and 36 rows to 4 in. square over st st, using size 2 needles

MATERIALS

1 x 2 oz. ball Jaeger Matchmaker 4-ply in shade 741 Mineral
1 pr size 2 needles

ABBREVIATIONS

alt – alternate • beg – beginning • cont – continue • dec – decrease • foll – following • inc – increase • k – knit • p – purl • patt – pattern • rem – remaining • rep – repeat • st(s) – stitch(es) • st st – stocking stitch • tog – together • yo – yarn over

FRONT
With size 2 needles, cast on 44 sts. Beg with a k row, work in st st until piece measures 7 in. from cast-on edge, ending with a wrong-side row.

BACK
With size 2 needles, pick up and k44 sts along the cast-on edge of front. Knit one row. Beginning with a k row, continue in st st and work as for front.

Transfer all sts to a holder or spare needle.

FLAP
With size 2 needles, cast on 8 sts.
K 1 row.
P 1 row.
Next row, begin increase:
Row 1: k2, yo, k4, yo, k2.
Row 2: p2, yo, p6, yo, p2.
Row 3: k2, yo, k8, yo, k2.
Row 4: p2, yo, p10, yo, p2.
Cont to increase in this way, working all new sts into st st until 44 sts.
Work 6 rows st st.
Transfer all stitches to a holder or spare needle.

STRAP
Make a twisted loop approximately 32 in. long, using four ends of yarn.

BUTTON LOOP
Make a sewn button loop at the button edge of the knitted flap.

TO FINISH

Bind off the sts for back and the sts for flap together using three needle bind offs with wrong sides facing to create a reverse seam.

Join side seams using your preferred sewing technique.

Sew button loop in place at bottom of flap and sew strap in place.

VARIATIONS

You can change the appearance of the bag by making a few basic alterations to the knitted flap.

Top right: Sew a twisted cord in two colors onto the edge of the flap.

Middle right: Sew a row of buttons along the bottom edge of the flap, or in patterns to create a button "flower."

Bottom right: Make a small flower and sew it to the flap of the bag.

Glossary

2-ply, 3-ply, 4-ply Knitting with two colors in the same row.

Backstitch A firm sewing stitch.

Binding off Fastening off stitches so they do not unravel.

Block, blocking Treating a piece of knitting to set its shape.

Bouclé yarn A fancy yarn with a knobbly effect.

Button band or **button border** A piece, knitted sideways or lengthwise, to which buttons are sewn.

Buttonhole band or **buttonhole border** A piece, knitted sideways or lengthwise, with buttonholes worked in as knitting proceeds.

Cable A group of stitches crossed over another group of stitches.

Cable needle A short, double-pointed knitting needle for working cables.

Casting on Making new stitches on a needle.

Chunky A heavy-weight yarn.

Circular needle A long, double-pointed knitting needle with a flexible center section, used for working in the round or for working large numbers of stitches.

Cuff The lower border of a sleeve.

Decreasing Working stitches together to reduce their number.

Double-pointed needle A knitting needle with a point at each end.

Duplicate stitch Another name for swiss darning.

Dye lot number Indicates the exact dye bath used to dye the yarn in question, not just the shade.

Ease The difference between the body measurement and the measurement of a garment.

Eyelet A small hole for a buttonhole or as part of a lace stitch pattern.

Fair Isle Knitting with two colors in the same row.

Fingering A fine-weight yarn (similar to 2-ply and 3-ply).

Float The strand of yarn left at the wrong side of the work when stranding.

Fully-fashioned shaping Shaping emphasized by working decreases (or increases) two or more stitches in from the edge of the work.

Garter stitch Formed by working all stitches as knit on every row, or all stitches as purl on every row.

Gauge The number of stitches and rows to a given measurement.

Hank A coil of yarn.

Increasing Making extra stitches.

Intarsia The technique of knitting pictures.

Knitwise As when knitting a stitch.

Long stitch A stitch made by wrapping the yarn twice around the needle.

Mattress stitch The stitch used for the invisible seam.

Multiple The number of stitches required for one pattern repeat.

Needle gauge A small metal or plastic sheet with holes of different sizes, labeled with needle sizes, for checking the size of knitting needles.

Pattern A stitch pattern or a set of instructions for making a garment.

Pattern repeat The stitches and rows that must be repeated to form a stitch pattern.

Point protector A plastic device to protect the point of a knitting needle.

Purlwise As when purling a stitch.

Raglan A sleeve and armhole shaping that slopes from the armhole to the neck edge.

Reverse stockinette stitch Stockinette stitch worked with the purl side as the right side.

Rib stitches or **ribbing** Various combinations of knit and purl stitches, arranged to form vertical lines.

Right and **left** (when describing parts of a garment) The terms that describe where the garment part will be when worn, e.g., the right sleeve is the sleeve worn on the right arm, not the sleeve on the right when the garment is viewed from the front.

Right side The side of the work that will be outside the garment when worn.

Ring marker A small split ring of metal or plastic, slipped onto a stitch or onto a needle to mark a particular position in the work.

Seam The join made when two pieces of knitting are sewn together.

Seed stitch A stitch pattern with a "dotted" appearance.

Selvage stitch The first or last stitch of a row worked in a different way than the rest of the row, to make a decorative edge or a firm, neat edge for seaming.

Set-in sleeve A sleeve and armhole shaping where the armhole is curved to take a curved sleeve head.

Shaping Increasing or decreasing the number of stitches to form the shape required.

Slip stitch A stitch slipped from one needle to the other without working into it, or a simple sewing stitch taking one strand from one edge and one strand from the other.

Stitch holder A device used for holding stitches temporarily.

Stockinette stitch Formed by working one row of knit stitches, one row of purl stitches, and repeating these two rows.

Swiss darning Embroidering over individual knitted stitches with another color.

Tapestry needle A sewing needle with a blunt tip and a large eye.

Twist A single stitch crossed over another stitch.

Twisting Carrying a color across the wrong side of several stitches in another color, twisting the two colors at intervals.

Worsted A medium-weight yarn (similar to double knitting).

Wrong side The side of the work that will be inside the garment when worn.

Index

PAGE NUMBERS IN ITALICS REFER TO ILLUSTRATIONS AND CAPTIONS.

Picture Credits & Acknowledgments

The material in this book previously appeared in:

All Stitched Up, by Jane Crowfoot

Designer Knits, by Ruth Maria Swepson

The Encyclopedia of Knitting, by Lesley Stanfield
and Melody Griffiths

The New Knitting Stitch Library, by Lesley Stanfield

Start Knitting, by Betty Barnden